AF698325

Economics in Film and Fiction

Milica Z. Bookman
and Aleksandra S. Bookman

Rowman & Littlefield Education
Lanham • New York • Toronto • Plymouth, UK

Published in the United States of America
by Rowman & Littlefield Education
A Division of Rowman & Littlefield Publishers, Inc.
A wholly owned subsidiary of The Rowman & Littlefield Publishing Group, Inc.
4501 Forbes Boulevard, Suite 200, Lanham, Maryland 20706
www.rowmaneducation.com

Estover Road
Plymouth PL6 7PY
United Kingdom

Copyright © 2009 by Milica Z. Bookman and Aleksandra S. Bookman

All rights reserved. No part of this publication may be reproduced, stored in a retrieval system, or transmitted in any form or by any means, electronic, mechanical, photocopying, recording, or otherwise, without the prior permission of the publisher.

British Library Cataloguing in Publication Information Available

Library of Congress Cataloging-in-Publication Data

Bookman, Milica Zarkovic.
Economics in film and fiction / Milica Z. Bookman and Aleksandra S. Bookman.
p. cm.
ISBN-13: 978-1-57886-961-9 (cloth : alk. paper)
ISBN-10: 1-57886-961-7 (cloth : alk. paper)
ISBN-13: 978-1-57886-962-6 (pbk. : alk. paper)
ISBN-10: 1-57886-962-5 (pbk. : alk. paper)
ISBN-13: 978-1-57886-963-3 (electronic)
ISBN-10: 1-57886-963-3 (electronic)
1. Economics—Study and teaching. 2. Economics—Study and teaching—Audio-visual aids. 3. Motion pictures in education. 4. Economics and literature. 5. Interdisciplinary approach in education. I. Bookman, Aleksandra S., 1987– II. Title.
HB74.5.B66 2009
330.071—dc22 2008034468

∞™ The paper used in this publication meets the minimum requirements of American National Standard for Information Sciences—Permanence of Paper for Printed Library Materials, ANSI/NISO Z39.48-1992.
Manufactured in the United States of America.

To Baka, Deda, and Oliver

Contents

Part III: Macroeconomic Topics

Acknowledgments

Milica:

My deepest gratitude goes to Thomas Burke, who has contributed to this project at each stage of its development. He helped out with class testing, discussion questions, and key concepts, and without fail, provided the sunshine that was so greatly appreciated. In addition, my thanks go to Ben Liebman, Cristian Pardo, Ann Zech and who were consistently available on short notice to answer a multitude of questions.

George Prendergast, Bill Madges, and Brice Wachterhauser provided the institutional support for professional meetings where this book material was presented. Paul Macolino and Alex Zebango worked under pressure to produce transparencies and DVDs for classroom use. Thank you.

Numerous people were involved in the selection of films and books. I am especially grateful to Andy Hine and Jennifer Hurst for the extensive lists they compiled as well as to Lee Tourscher who sought out economic concepts in selected novels. I am also grateful to Lisa Baglione, Mike Fergueson, Lynn Holmes, and Christina Rennhoff for their contribution to the final selection of titles.

The following helped out with the administration of the questionnaire that tested student familiarity with film and book titles: Thomas Burke, Dori Pappas, Cristina Rennhoff, and Yue Fan. Thank you all.

When exorbitant permission costs threatened the project, Tony Joes, Ben Liebman, and Cristian Pardo brainstormed and helped me think out of the box. I am also grateful to Elizabeth Fenjves and Stephen Urice whose understanding of intellectual property issues helped me get my bearings and whose friendship helped me move on.

To Sarah Dorger, thank you for your enthusiasm. Tori Olson, Michelle Lockard, Serina Foehr, and Matt Early—your efforts on behalf of this project are greatly appreciated.

The material in this book was class-tested at Saint Joseph's University during two semesters: fall 2007 and spring 2008. I am grateful to all the students in my introductory macroeconomics classes, especially those who were motivated to watch additional films and read additional books to make suggestions for title inclusions.

Thanks are also due to Tom Koerner who has always been accommodating and prompt in addressing publishing concerns, as well as to Maera Winters for her assistance.

My passion for films and literature developed over many decades. There are many people who have contributed along the way. I have benefited from Andy Hine's love of classic movies and contemporary literature. Nenad Amodaj provided a constant stream of ideas about existential films and books. My father Slobodan Zarkovic instilled in me an appreciation for westerns while my mother Danica Zarkovic gave me a love for Russian nineteenth-century classics. Paolo Ceratto awakened my interest in Italian cinema of the 1950s and 1960s.

Over the past two years Aleksandra and I have relied heavily on the use of Netflix for a constant stream of videos as well as Blockbuster-Mariposa Plaza for quick runs to check film scenes. We have also benefited greatly from the embracing atmosphere of Books and Books (in Coral Gables) where we spent many an afternoon browsing through novels. Our gratitude to Mitch Kaplan for providing such an environment is huge.

A million thank yous to Richard and Karla for providing the emotional anchor so essential for a project of this magnitude. Richard's contribution to this book has been comprehensive and invaluable, ranging from scene suggestions to technical expertise. The memory of Richard holed up in a Caribbean hotel room revising the final draft of the manuscript will stay with me forever.

Finally, Aleksandra. Without you, this book would not have happened. You gave me a different perspective; you opened creative worlds unknown to me. You took me into your subculture and patiently explained. Even before we began working on this project, your contribution to my lectures was undeniable. Over the course of many dinnertime conversations, the boundaries between the latest films, your required school readings, and the principles of economics became blurred. My next-day lectures inevitably acquired a youthful spin. And after the book idea was born, we learned to work together and to complement each other. In illness and in health, we persevered as a team, relentlessly forging forward. Once when we presented *Economics in Film and Fiction* at a conference, a question from the audience was prefaced with the following words to me:

"The secret of your success is Aleksandra." But I knew that already, and I am grateful beyond words.

Aleksandra:

I don't think I'll be writing a book any time soon so I'm going to go ahead and thank *some* people now just in case I never get another chance:

- My amazing family: Karla—I could not have imagined a better role model growing up. You've taught me everything I know about being street-smart and surviving in New York City. You've shown that it's possible to be both smart and pretty at the same time. You're my best friend. Daddy—I give you a hard time, but you know I think you're funny (kind of). Well, at least you have the oversized brain and contagious geniality to make up for it. I thank you both so much for everything from diaper changes to *Economics in Film and Fiction* and everything in between.
- So maybe it's a little clichéd to acknowledge my boyfriend, but I think four years merits at least a *tiny* nod in his direction. Cyrill, I appreciate how much you've gone through just to keep me happy. You are like no one I know.
- Elisa Rodriguez-Vila: what haven't you helped me through in life?? This book was no exception. To my roommate in life, thank you.
- Natalie Aghion: love at first sight. And you're also a Stern Business School student, which means you help me with my Econ. You're the best.
- To my Miami girls: Elyse, Hillary, Christina, and Rachel. Through the years we've gotten to know each other in ways that show true friendship. It is so great having you girls to come home to. Thank you for the times. And putting up with my absence while writing this book.
- Taylor Withers: although not as frequent anymore, late-night brainstorming with you is always a pleasure.
- To my ladies of Roma: Jan, Kate, Michele, Elisa, and Casey. Maybe you did not directly affect this book (probably hindered its progress), but what you really did for me I could never even put into words.
- With all my schooling, my brain has become an investment all on its own. A thank-you to those of you who molded it:
    - RE Middle: Ms. Collasso, Mr. Peterson, Ms. Denson, Mr. Lambert, Ms. Onorati, Mr. Bott, Mr. Brown, Mr. Kappelman, Ms. Mendoza, and Mr. Walach
    - RE High: Ms. Szolodko, Ms. Bustamante, Ms. Borona, Ms. Lester, Sr. Urbina, Sra. Mestre, Mr. Mac, Joe Ackner, Doc Weiser, Ms. Novitski,

Coach Brenner, Ms. Miller, Mr. Felipe, Ms. Chandler, Mr. Hewett, Ms. Proenza, Mr. Rodriguez, Ms. Sulkes, and O.P.

  - NYU: Professors Trace Jordan, Cole, DB, Badal, Peters, and Daughtry
  - Abroad: In Rome: Professori Argentieri, Hansen, Antomarini, D'Agostino. In Cannes: Raju and Cedric

- Alex Trebek: no, really—the sassy comments, French accents, and Double Jeopardy helped me write this book.
- And finally my amazing mother: I am sad that the process of this book is over. It was a wonderful bonding experience that not only taught me a lot about economics, but also about the type of person I hope to be one day. I have never known anyone so smart, strong, determined, or beautiful. I want to thank you so much for everything you have ever given me, but I would not even know where to start because the list is endless. But I do know that the time I have spent with you is #1 and always will be.

Introduction

Many people have read *Charlotte's Web* and watched *The Wizard of Oz* when they were young. However, when they think of those childhood stories, chances are it's not the economics principles that they remember. And yet, decisions about Wilber's fate are based on opportunity cost, and Templeton the Rat responds to economic incentives. Similarly, Dorothy follows "the yellow brick road" that is made of precious metal, and the Scarecrow's transformation has to do with human capital. Also, these same people probably didn't read *The Iliad* and wonder about the production costs of building the Trojan Horse nor watch *Legally Blonde* and focus on the price of Elle's shoes.

The fact is that people have consistently been exposed to economics principles in the movies they've watched and the books they've read. We have written *Economics in Film and Fiction* to help people recognize those principles. This book provides an innovative lens through which to observe principles of economics and as such, it bridges the world of academic economics with Hollywood and literature.

To make this bridge effective and relevant, we used a broad range of films and fiction. The compilation of the book list began with an overview of some high school reading lists and childhood favorites (hence the inclusion of *Catcher in the Rye* as well as *Snow White and the Seven Dwarfs*). To those, contemporary bestsellers were added (such as *The Da Vinci Code*) as well as some popular classics (*Gulliver's Travels* and *The Odyssey*). Film choices were initially made with an informal polling of student residents in a freshman dormitory at New York University. Student recognition of titles, actors, and authors was gauged using a questionnaire administered to some six hundred students in introductory economics classes at Saint

Joseph's University. As a follow-up, we compared Facebook's compilation of the most popular movies watched on U.S. campuses was compared to our list.

By seeing how often economics principles appear in popular and classic films and books, readers will come to believe that economics really is everywhere. Indeed, after watching Brad Pitt make consumption decisions based on his diminishing marginal utility or reading Charles Dickens's description of food shortages, readers will make the connection between theory and the real world.

Economics in Film and Fiction consists of thirty-three self-contained chapters that correspond to specific economic topics. The order in which the topics are presented does not follow the order used by any particular textbook; therefore, the book can be used to supplement any textbook. Each chapter begins with a list of key concepts that are then illustrated in selected film scenes and fiction passages. The film scenes and fiction passages are described, and the economic concepts therein are explained.

The organization of the chapters maximizes flexibility and enables readers to easily pick and choose to suit their tastes and course goals. Readers need not be film buffs or literature pros to use illustrations from *Economics in Film and Fiction* as the material is simple and self-explanatory. Some may choose to assign only films or only fiction, depending on their personal inclinations. However, by reading both for each topic, the universality of economic themes is more clearly recognized.

Every chapter engages readers with questions that catapult them into the real world. The questions serve to make the connection from the film scene or book passage to real businesses, industries, and economic activities.

The authors of *Economics in Film and Fiction* are a college professor and a college student. The participation of the student, a member of the same demographic cohort that provides the book's principal readers, lends a youthful perspective, one that is reflected in the choice of films and readings as well as the assignment questions that interpret their content. It is her link to youth culture, as well as her knowledge of the entertainment industry and its characters, which provides an indispensable perspective for this project.

Finally, some words of caution. The description of some scenes necessitated poetic license in order to set the framework for illustration of economic content. Also, although every attempt was made to avoid spoilers, they were inevitable in some film and book descriptions.

I

GENERAL TOPICS

Chapter 1

Rational Behavior and Economic Incentives

Film: *JAWS*
Fiction: *THE SCARLET LETTER*

KEY ECONOMIC CONCEPTS

Economists have identified several principles that describe people's behavior. One of these states that people behave rationally when they seek to achieve their goals. The concept of *rational behavior* implies that people consider all their options and make the best possible decision based on those options.

Another economic principle that describes human behavior states that people respond to *economic incentives*. A higher wage will induce a worker to change jobs, and a sale will induce a consumer to buy a coat. In responding to economic incentives, people pursue their *self-interest*. Adam Smith, known as the father of economics, wrote extensively about self-interest, stating that when individuals pursue it, and are unfettered in their pursuit, the result is beneficial for both the individual as well as society at large.

In order to behave rationally and to respond to economic incentives, it is assumed that people have *perfect information* about all relevant variables. Without it, they cannot make informed decisions.

JAWS

Rated PG/1975/124 min /Roy Scheider, Richard Dreyfuss, Lorraine Gary
Directed by Steven Spielberg
Winner of three Academy Awards including Best Original Score

A young woman is attacked by a shark, and her body washes up on an Amity Island beach. Police Chief Brody (Roy Scheider) wants to close down the beaches but meets with resistance from the town's mayor who is concerned with the negative impact on the island's businesses. The mayor has his way, and the shark claims more victims. An out-of-town shark specialist, Matt Hooper (Richard Dreyfuss) shows up. He and Brody share a desire to catch the shark, and so their friendship develops. The town posts a prize for the fisherman who catches the Great White that continues to terrorize the oceans. While numerous fishermen try to capture it, only Quint (Robert Shaw) knows enough about sharks and has the equipment to be a serious contender for the prize. One day he sets out, together with Brody and Hooper, to face the shark. A tense battle on open seas ensues. Not everyone returns.

Economic Concepts In Jaws

Scene 4 (0:00–2:09)/ Minutes 11:21–13:30

Preparations for the July 4th parade are in full swing on Amity Island, and eager townsfolk await the onslaught of tourists that will come off the ferries from the mainland. Underlying their mood is the expectation of a successful summer, one in which a large number of tourists spend a large amount of money in local businesses. On this perfect summer day, it seems that nothing can dampen the people's jubilance. That is because they do not know about the shark attack.

Police Chief Brody knows. He has just returned from viewing the remains of last night's shark victim, and there is no doubt in his mind—beachgoers must be warned of the danger lurking just off the coast. They must be kept out of the water until the killer shark is caught. Brody is a careful, risk-adverse man, so he instructs his staff to post "No Swimming" signs along the beaches. But when Amity Island's mayor realizes what the police chief intends to do, his reaction is immediate and unequivocal. With an urgent stride, he seeks out Brody throughout the town. He wants to prevent the beach closing because he believes it would lead to an economic disaster.

The mayor explains that Amity Island is a tourist destination and as such, its residents depend on tourist spending. He means that most of them work in the tourism industry. They own bed-and-breakfasts or motels. They run restaurants and coffee shops. They bartend in the evenings, sell suntan lotion at the pharmacy, rent their boats for fishing trips, and drive taxis. Responding to economic incentives, they have developed their businesses to cater to tourists. If the beaches close, word of the deadly attack will spread and panic will ensue. Tourists already on the island will rapidly depart while those still to arrive will cancel their reservations and make alternate plans. Without tourist dollars, the island's residents receive no revenue or income. And since their businesses are seasonal, they have no possibility of recovering their losses during the winter. A decrease in standards of living looms in their future.

For all these reasons, the mayor believes he is acting in the best interests of the town when he insists on keeping the beaches open (he is also acting in his own self-interest since a disgruntled, unemployed, and impoverished town population is unlikely to forget their troubles at reelection time). The mayor is behaving rationally.

But Brody is also behaving rationally when he suggests closing down the beaches. The image of the shark victim's severed body parts is still vivid in his mind. He knows those huge bites were not made by a baby shark but rather by an oversized predator who, having tasted blood, is very likely to strike again. This reality leads Brody to focus on preventing additional tragedies. Like the mayor, he too is considering the economic implications as he figures two shark attacks will be more damaging for the town than one. Brody is considering the long term implications of shark attacks while the mayor is thinking about the short term, namely the holiday weekend.

And so, two rational men, both claiming to represent the best interests of Amity Island, face off against the background of bucolic coves and children splashing innocently in shallow waters. How do they reconcile their differences?

The deadlock is broken when the town doctor chimes in. This little bespectacled man is the physician who performed the autopsy on the shark victim, the same one who pointedly noted the oversized jaw bite that left its mark on the victim. Under pressure from the mayor, that same doctor has now changed his position and is stating that the young woman died in a boating accident. A boating accident! In the face of such united pressure from the town's most eminent citizens, Brody backs down and agrees to keep the beaches open.

The dubious alliance between the mayor and the doctor has, in addition to pressuring Brody, served to suppress, manipulate, and alter information. Both the townspeople and the tourists are denied information on which to base their decision to swim in the ocean. As it turns out, controlling information was not possible for very long in *Jaws*. On a huge billboard advertising beaches on Amity Island, a prankster drew a shark fin just above the water line, conveying clear information about the perils of the town's beaches.

Discussion Questions

1. Cancun, Orlando, and Aspen are vacation towns where the tourist industry plays a huge economic role. What kind of disaster would be a *Jaws* equivalent in those towns, and how would each economy be affected?
2. A tsunami hit the beach resorts of Thailand in 2004. Given what you know about the economic effects of a shark attack on Amity Island, what do you think were the economic consequences of the tsunami? How are the two disasters the same, how are they different?
3. After a second shark attack on Amity Island, regional newspapers and local television stations picked up the story. On film, as in real world tourist resorts, negative news carries negative economic consequences. If you worked for a PR firm representing Amity Island, how would you minimize the impact of the shark?

THE SCARLET LETTER

By Nathaniel Hawthorne
New York: Pocket Books, 1994

This story takes place in Puritan New England in the late seventeeth century, a time of strict codes of personal conduct. Hester Prynne has committed adultery with a man she refuses to identify and has thus incurred the wrath of the town's leaders. For punishment, she is put in jail for three months and then forced to wear a scarlet-colored letter A (for adulteress) on her dress. Nevertheless, Hester manages to survive this shame and sets up an embroidery business in order to support herself. With the passing of time, Hester becomes accustomed to her life, and the town becomes forgiving and accepting. It is the Reverend Dimmesdale who cannot live with his guilt—he was her lover, and yet he kept quiet about it, allowing her to take all the blame. When Hester's long absent husband Roger Chillingworth shows up, he takes his anger out on Dimmesdale.

Economic Concepts in *The Scarlet Letter*

pp. 82–83

After spending three months confined to a prison, Hester Prynne is released and has to find a way to support herself and her baby daughter. Since she is a skilled seamstress, she decides to sew for the community and offer her embroidery for sale. But she worries that no one will hire her or buy her work. She is, after all, a convicted adulteress.

It turns out that the villagers do want to buy her embroidery. In fact, they flock to her, seeking out her services. In addition to women's Sunday best, Hester's handiwork shows up on the clothes of military men, ministers, babies, brides, and even the governor. When village women lined up to buy Hester's embroidery, were they just curious to see, close up, a woman who had sinned? Were they moved to commiserate with her? Or did they simply like a style that was light, airy, intricate, and bold, in such contrast to the austere New England environment in which it was produced.

Whatever their motivation, the fact is that Hester had more clients than she could handle as her embroidery became the latest fashion and everyone wanted to own it. And as Hester pursued her self-interest, the more she sewed, the more she sold, and the more income she earned.

When Hester emerged from prison, she made a decision to stay in town at least for the short run, long enough to see if she could support herself. She reevaluated her decision to stay several times. The more time went by and the greater her new celebrity status, Hester's decision not to relocate to an anonymous city increasingly seemed a rational one. Given her earnings, staying in town, despite the shame, indicates she responded to economic incentives.

Perfect information about Hester's adultery was at the root of her business success. The blazing scarlet letter A that she was forced to wear on her dress provided immediate and unmistakable information to anyone who saw her.

Discussion Questions

1. Comment: Hester's adultery made her embroidery more desirable, just like scandal helped Madonna sell her records and Paris Hilton sell her perfume.
2. Centuries after Hester wore the letter A on her clothes, many people voluntarily wear letters such as G, A, and P on their T-shirts. What kind of information do these letters convey?
3. By contemporary standards, the public display of Hester's sins on her clothing seems harsh. Yet in some parts of the United States, residents are informed when a convicted child molester moves to their neighborhood. Comment: Both are effective ways of ensuring perfect information.

Chapter 2

Scarcity, Choice, and Opportunity Cost

Film: *LEGALLY BLONDE*
Fiction: *THE ODYSSEY*

KEY ECONOMIC CONCEPTS

The concept of *scarcity* is fundamental to the study of economics. There are not enough resources for all of us to have what we want. Indeed, human wants are unlimited while the resources to achieve those wants are limited. Since we cannot have everything, we have to make *choices* about what we want and need (consumers choose what to buy given their income, firms choose which goods to produce given their inputs, governments choose which programs to support given their revenue).

When choices are made, one outcome is picked over another. That involves a *trade-off*, namely trading off one good for another. Buying more of one good means buying less of another. The value of what is given up is called the *opportunity cost*. In this way, the cost of a decision is measured in terms of the foregone opportunity to choose the best alternative.

How do individuals (and firms and governments) decide which outcome to choose? They weigh the benefits of each action against the costs of that action. If costs are lower than benefits, then they will pursue the action; if costs are higher, they won't. This is called *cost-benefit analysis*.

Economists believe that rational individuals make choices *on the margin*, meaning that they look at the extra, additional benefit (or cost) of a decision. Most choices are not all-or-nothing but rather entail decisions about incremental activity (for example, the consumption of one more drink or the production of one more automobile). Decision-making on the margin implies that *marginal costs* are weighed against *marginal benefits*.

LEGALLY BLONDE

Rated PG13/2001/1hr 36min//Reese Witherspoon, Luke Wilson
Directed by Robert Luketic

Elle Woods (Reese Witherspoon) is a popular sorority queen on a California college campus. With no troubles or ambitions, she focuses on her manicures, her accessories, and her boyfriend, Warner Huntington III. As he prepares to attend Harvard Law School, Warner breaks up with Elle, telling her she is insufficiently serious to be a lawyer's wife. This shocks Elle into action, and she too applies to Harvard. Despite her unconventional application, she gets accepted and sets off to win her boyfriend back. Elle is not a traditional Harvard attendee and at first, both students and faculty ridicule her. However, Elle turns out to be smarter than she appears. She succeeds in winning the respect of her peers and the love of Emmett (Luke Wilson).

Economic Concepts in *Legally Blonde*

Scene 3 (3:46–5:04)/ Minutes 9:02–10:19

It was supposed to be the happiest day of Elle's life. Warner invited her to a romantic restaurant where, she believed, he would tenderly reach for her hand and propose they get married. In expectation of this scenario, Elle takes extra care to look her best, spending the day fussing over her hair and nails and picking out just the right dress: it has to be the right color to complement her skin tone and the right cut to accentuate her silhouette. Above all, she has to pick the right shoes: a strappy pair of stilettos. Elle thinks shoes are crucial for the image she wants to convey on this important day.

With a champagne glass in hand, Warner tells Elle he wants to discuss their future. He explains that he comes from a family of five generations of senators, that he too wants to be a senator by the age of thirty, and therefore, he must become more serious. That means, rather than marry Elle, he needs to break up with her. While smiling at her, Warner says she is simply not an appropriate wife for a future senator.

Elle does not know if she heard correctly. Warner can't be smiling while ruining her life, right? She cries, whimpering loudly as her cheeks blacken from her watering mascara. Her shock turns to anger as she raises her voice and storms out of the restaurant. All eyes are on the embarrassed

Warner as he rushes out to catch up with her. After retrieving his luxury convertible, he finally locates Elle hobbling home by foot on her high heels. She will not look at him as he drives alongside her, coaxing her into the car. He calls out terms of endearment that Elle ignores, holding her head high and walking, wobbling on her super high heels. He softens his voice and tries again. It is only when he says, "You'll ruin your shoes," that Elle stops, thinks for a moment, and opens the car door to slip inside.

Elle changes her mind because she makes the following calculation. Her sorority is over an hour's walk from the restaurant. The road, although paved, is uneven and hilly. Her high heels are not intended for walking, just for looking pretty. Not only will her feet hurt if she walks home but, more importantly, the shoes will be ruined. The straps will break, the leather will tear, and the heels will become scruffy. They will be beyond repair and will have to be replaced. They are very expensive shoes, and Elle knows their exact replacement cost, assuming they can be replaced. On the other hand, Elle has her pride and does not want to swallow it.

Elle cannot save her shoes as well as her dignity. In order to get back to her sorority, Elle has to choose between walking (and give up her stilettos) or accepting Warner's ride (and give up her self-respect). By choosing to get in the car, she trades off her self-respect. The opportunity cost she incurs is the value of her lost dignity, a subjective calculation that only she can make, at a value that only she can estimate.

Moreover, Elle is thinking on the margin. She is not considering never walking again or ruining all her shoes. Rather, she is considering the cost of one additional hour of walking relative to the cost of spending an additional ten minutes in the car with Warner.

In this way, shoes play a crucial role in Elle's decision not to walk home (as they do again in the final scenes of the movie when Elle's knowledge of shoe fashion helps her argument in court). Her inclination toward expensive shoes affects her behavior as she probably would not have accepted Warner's ride if she had been wearing sneakers that can take wear and tear. But there are many women like Elle whose self-image is tied to wearing expensive shoes, such as Manolo Blahniks or Jimmy Choos, to the delight of the luxury shoe industry.

Discussion Questions

1. Elle is passionate about shoes and likes to keep up with the latest fashions. The booming shoe industry counts on women like Elle. By frequently changing shoe styles, the shoe industry forces women like Elle to make choices. What are those choices, and how do they affect the shoe industry?

2. Marriage proposals in restaurants are common, and an engagement ring buried in a dessert has often been depicted on film. If you were a

groom, why would you choose to pop the question in a restaurant? What would your cost-benefit analysis be? What would your trade-offs be?

3. When Warner breaks up with Elle, she begins shouting at him. Use economic concepts to explain why the restaurant staff is concerned when Elle makes a scene. Would they be equally concerned if a celebrity such as Kate Hudson created a scene?

THE ODYSSEY

By Homer
New York: Farrar, Straus and Giroux, 1998

It has been some twenty years since Odysseus left his homeland in Ithaca. At first he was at war, fighting in the Greek army to return Helen of Troy to her husband. Then, on his way back home he had numerous adventures and mishaps that kept him away for another decade. He spent some time with Circe (whose sorcery turned his sailors into pigs), the Cyclops (who ate some of his men), and Kalypso (who gave him a tour of the underworld). All the while his faithful wife Penelope was raising their son and trying to keep evil suitors from taking over his property. In order to stall them, she said she would pick one to marry only after she finished weaving her tapestry. But in secret, every night she undid what she had weaved during the day, all the while hoping for Odysseus's return. When he did finally reach his homeland, Odysseus disguised himself as a beggar and succeeded in reclaiming his rightful place at Penelope's side.

Economic Concepts in *The Odyssey*

p. 87

Although he has spent many years with the beautiful and immortal Kalypso, Odysseus is anxious to return to his native Ithaca. His impatience has reached unbearable levels, and he consistently dreams of his homeland with the rugged coastline and abundant olive groves. He also dreams of his wife Penelope, whom he still loves dearly. Odysseus was once a wealthy man, respected in the community. On Kalypso's island, he has nothing.

Despite his dreams of returning home, Odysseus remains trapped. He cannot set out on the journey home without Kalypso's endorsement and assistance. Only she can help him build a ship, organize a crew, and secure the necessary provisions.

Unfortunately, Kalypso's love for Odysseus has obscured her vision and has led her to consistently dismiss his unhappiness. This situation would have continued if it weren't for Zeus, the god of gods, who heard of Odysseus's distress and ordered Kalypso to release him. Although she knows she must obey, Kalypso nevertheless makes one final desperate attempt to convince Odysseus to voluntarily stay with her. She proposes a trade: if he stays, she will make him immortal.

Now Odysseus has to make a choice. He cannot become immortal and at the same time return to Ithaca. If he chooses immortality, he will live forever but it will be alongside Kalypso. Her love and godly powers will ensure he is protected and want for nothing. If, on the other hand, he chooses to leave, he will undoubtedly die in the near future, as he is already a middle-aged man, and there are no guarantees that he will ever reach Penelope.

Odysseus compares the opportunity cost of giving up immortality to the opportunity cost of giving up his wife's love and his agricultural earnings in Ithaca. He weighs living with Kalypso forever versus living with Penelope for a shorter time. He decides to return home.

Odysseus's choice is based on imperfect information. He has no idea if his wife, believing him lost at sea, remarried in his absence. He has no idea if his home has been sold and his possessions dispersed. Perhaps there has been a deadly war in Ithaca, or perhaps an earthquake swallowed up the entire island. It turns out that Kalypso, a goddess who can see into the future, has information that, according to the laws of the gods, she cannot share with a mortal such as Odysseus. Kalypso knows Odysseus will face huge adversity on the seas as he works his way home. He will lose his men and will barely survive. He will be famished and will suffer great pain. Had that same information been available to Odysseus, he might have altered his decision. Instead he makes a choice in the absence of perfect information.

Discussion Questions

1. Before making a decision to undergo a dangerous voyage home, Odysseus weighs his expected costs and benefits. Similarly, before deciding to enlist in the army and serve in Iraq, young Americans weigh their expected costs and benefits. Describe those costs and benefits, including the opportunity costs.

2. How would Odysseus's choice have been affected if he could have e-mailed Penelope (to see if she had remarried in his absence) or watched CNN (to learn if there had been a war in Ithaca)?

3. Odysseus has to consider the danger of his upcoming sea voyage and the high probability that he will not survive it. Safety during travel is a key consideration in his decision-making. Safety is also a concern in modern transportation industries. When automakers install seatbelts, what are they trading off for greater safety? What are the passengers trading off when they decide not to fasten their seat belts?

Chapter 3
Markets

Film: *CASABLANCA*
Fiction: *PRIDE AND PREJUDICE*

KEY ECONOMIC CONCEPTS

Economists use the term *market* to define the interaction between *buyers and sellers* of a particular good or service. Anywhere and anyhow buyers and sellers come together, a market is said to exist. Households and firms interact in markets by trading. All markets are governed by institutional arrangements that dictate how trade between buyers and sellers takes place.

The *product market* includes buyers and sellers of a particular *good* (such as a refrigerator) and *service* (such as medical treatment). There is also the *factor market*, in which *factors of production* are bought and sold. These include *labor, land, capital,* and *entrepreneurship*. These factors are also known as *inputs* in the production process, and the *outputs* of that process are the goods and services that are produced.

CASABLANCA

Rated PG/1943/1hr 43min/Humphrey Bogart, Ingrid Bergman
Directed by Michael Curtiz
Winner of three Academy Awards, including Best Picture and Director

This film takes place during World War II in Casablanca, Morocco. The city is not occupied by the Nazis, and it offers one of the few routes to the United States still open to Europeans fleeing Europe. Rick Blaine (Humphrey Bogart) is an American who owns Rick's Café, the most popular restaurant in town. It is actually more than a restaurant. It is the place where everybody gathers to people-watch and conduct business. It is here that refugees from Europe try to obtain exit papers so they can board one of the few boats or planes that will get them to freedom. Both German officials and French authorities suspect what is happening but never have enough proof to stop it. When Rick's former girlfriend Ilsa (Ingrid Bergman) shows up, seeking exit papers for her new husband, Rick has to make some difficult choices.

Economic Concepts in *Casablanca*

Scene 4 (0:00–1:32)/ Minutes 6:30–8:02

Just a few black-and-white minutes of *Casablanca* portray economic activity across a broad range of markets. The scene is inside Rick's Café, where elegant people come and go while Sam, the piano player, entertains the crowd. On the surface, it seems like any evening, in any restaurant, anywhere.

In reality, at each table some kind of business is conducted since each person in the restaurant is a buyer and/or a seller. Trade in the product market happens when a man walks up to the bar and orders a drink (in exchange for money) while another negotiates two letters of transit out of Casablanca (in exchange for money). Trade also happens in the factor market as workers are hired to perform various jobs associated with the restaurant business (the piano player entertains guests, waiters serve diners, and cooks prepare meals). Rick has rented the physical space that houses the restaurant (land), he has purchased stoves and coffee machines (capital), and he has ingeniously provided the only location in Casablanca that simultaneously satisfies several needs of the city's residents (entrepreneurship).

In a back room of Rick's Café, people gather quietly to gamble, their silk gowns and formal jackets rubbing against each other as they huddle over a table. Gambling represents a trade in services, as people are buying excitement, risk, and the opportunity to win.

In addition to the product and factor markets, Rick's Café is also a market for information. In its high-ceiling rooms and alcoves, well-to-do refugees from Nazi-controlled Europe get crucial information on ways to get out of Casablanca and on to the United States. Spies get information about the German presence in town, and single men and women get information about who is still single (such information is often traded indirectly as payment is made for the drink or meal that justifies one's presence in the Café where information flows).

At one point, an elegant woman, who has obviously come upon hard times, goes to Rick's Café in order to raise some cash. There she meets a local buyer, and she offers to sell her ornate diamond bracelet. At first he brushes her off, saying, "Everyone here sells diamonds. There are diamonds everywhere!" His words do not imply that there is no market for diamonds in Casablanca. To the contrary, there is a vibrant diamond market, and he is one of its chief buyers and sellers. Rather, he is establishing an advantageous negotiating position and preparing to offer a low price. The bracelet is thus traded in the market as used jewelry for much less cash than the desperate lady had hoped to receive.

Discussion Questions

1. College cafeterias are similar to Rick's Café insofar as they provide a market for more than just meals. Can you identify some product and factor markets in a college cafeteria? Also, what kind of information is traded there?
2. In Rick's Café, a man sells tickets for a ship voyage out of Casablanca. Why does he only accept cash. Can you think of contemporary markets that operate only with cash?
3. Gambling was a lucrative business in Rick's Café as it is today in Las Vegas and Atlantic City. There continues to be a market for gambling even if most gamblers lose money. Is gambling a rational behavior?

PRIDE AND PREJUDICE

By Jane Austen
New York: Tor Books, 1994

This is a story of love and marriage in nineteenth-century England. Mrs. Bennet lives with her five unmarried daughters. Her primary goal is to find them all wealthy husbands. Although the daughters would prefer to fall in love, they don't entirely object to arranged marriages as this is the custom of their times. In addition, they are under pressure to marry because, according to the terms of their great grandfather's will, their house, land, and the income from it one day will go to a relative since their father did not produce male heirs. The book focuses on Elizabeth, one of the daughters who has a protracted love/hate relationship with Mr. Darcy, the town's most eligible bachelor.

Economic Concepts in *Pride and Prejudice*

pp. 1–3

The Bennet family lives in rural Hertfordshire where rolling green hills inspire peace and serenity. That peace is broken one day when a young and wealthy man, Mr. Bingley, moves to town. Everyone is ablaze with this news since there are numerous unmarried young women looking for proposals. His presence introduces new possibilities and upsets the preexisting balance between buyers and sellers in the marriage market.

It is a market because there are single young women and single young men in the same town, and they are seeking to come together to make a trade (namely, to marry). In nineteenth-century British society, they do not meet at the local bar or at a sports event. Rather, most marriages are at least partially arranged by parents who nudge their children into chaperoned social events that will maximize their opportunities of meeting an appropriate spouse. Parental involvement through such events constitutes the institutional arrangements that define how trade between buyers and traders takes place.

The marriage market in Hertfordshire is characterized by an imbalance between the sexes. There are more young women in town than young men. The men have more career options so they move to London and other big cities to work, while the girls do not leave home until they marry. This discrepancy between the sexes causes the competition for the men to be fierce. Sometimes the imbalance is adjusted by migration as when a young man, such as Mr. Bingley (and later, his friend Mr. Darcy), moves into town. When that happens, it shows that the marriage market is dynamic and not limited by local supply.

Who are the buyers and who are the sellers in this marriage market? The reader gets the impression that the young women are the buyers since it is their mothers who are most actively seeking out marriage proposals. The social-climbing Mrs. Bennet is a good example. When the story begins, she has five single daughters and not one proposal in sight. Jane Austin writes on page one that the business of Mrs. Bennet's life is to get her daughters married. However, not just any union will do—she has to arrange good partnerships for them to men who are stable and who have means and future prospects to provide for their wives. Mrs. Bennet is rational. She is trying to maximize the wealth that her daughters achieve through marriage, believing that wealth leads to happiness.

Thus when Mr. Bingley shows up in town, Mrs. Bennet must work quickly and elbow her way into his presence so he can develop an interest in one of her daughters. It does not matter which daughter—the sweet one, the fun-loving one, the brilliant one, the studious one, or the flighty one—as long as one of them snags him before Hertfordshire's other single women attract his attention. By meeting him before the other families do, Mrs. Bennet will give her daughters an advantage in the marriage market.

But how does Mrs. Bennet know if Mr. Bingley has sufficient means to satisfy her requirements? She makes it her business to collect all available information so she can judge the value of the total package that he is selling (that is, himself). Similar information is customarily made available about dowries, namely the assets brought into the marriage by the bride. Information about net worth is openly discussed in nineteenth-century British society (everyone knows, for example, that Mr. Darcy has annual earnings of 10,000 British pounds). Every family's assets and possessions are known by anyone who cares to inquire. Such transparency is necessary to conduct marriage negotiations on a level playing field so that all participants—the buyers and the sellers—have perfect information. In this way, the relative advantages and disadvantages in the negotiations are open knowledge.

Discussion Questions

1. If Mrs. Bennet is successful in her efforts with Mr. Bingley, the end result will be a lavish wedding. In nineteenth-century England, like in contemporary United States, such formal celebrations of marriage have come to be about more than love and a legal document. They have come to be about numerous product and factor markets. In addition to the clothing market (where the wedding dress is purchased), which other product and factor markets are involved in a wedding?
2. In what way are eighteenth-century mothers similar to contemporary professional matchmakers and online dating services? Who are the buyers and who are the sellers in contemporary dating markets? Why don't modern singles save on the matchmaking fee and allow well-meaning parents to arrange their marriages as it was done in *Pride and Prejudice*?
3. According to a stipulation passed down through the generations, Mr. Bennet is penalized because he did not produce a male heir and so, upon his death, his family loses the right to the ancestral home and lands. Which markets will be affected by this stipulation after Mr. Bennet passes away?

Chapter 4

Supply and Demand

Film: *DIE ANOTHER DAY*
Fiction: *THE SNEETCHES*

KEY ECONOMIC CONCEPTS

The concepts of demand and supply are at the core of economics. *Demand* refers to the willingness and ability to buy specific quantities of a good at varying prices. In other words, it is the term economists use to describe how buyers react to different prices that are presented to them in a market. The *law of demand* states that the quantity demanded is always inversely related to the price of the goods. Normally, buyers buy less of a good when its price is high and more when its price is low. Individual demand refers to a single person while *market demand* describes the entire industry at any point in time.

There are several *determinants of demand*, including taste, income, availability and price of other goods, expectations about future prices and income, and the number of buyers. These influence buyers to buy what they buy. Meanwhile, price is the only *determinant of the quantity demanded*.

Economists distinguish between different kinds of goods sold in markets, depending on how demand for them changes as the buyer's income changes. *Normal goods* are those for which demand increases when income rises while *inferior goods* are those for which demand decreases when income increases. Economists are also interested in seeing how demand for a good changes when the price of related goods change. For this reason, they distinguish between *complements* and *substitutes.* The former are goods that are typically demanded together, for example tennis rackets and tennis balls, while the latter, given that they are goods used for the same purposes, typically are not demanded together. Examples of substitutes include tea and coffee. With goods that are complements, a change in the price of one good will cause the demand for the complementary good to change in the opposite direction. If the goods are substitutes, then the change in the price of one will send the demand for its substitute in the same direction.

In addition to demand, every market by definition also contains supply. *Supply* refers to the willingness and ability to offer specific quantities of a good at varying prices. Supply is the word economists use to describe how the sellers react to different prices presented to them in the market. According to the *law of supply,* the relationship between the price of a good and its quantity supplied is direct, in other words, as price goes up, suppliers will supply more. As with demand, economists distinguish between *individual* and *market supply.*

There are several *determinants of supply,* including technology, factor prices, profitability of other product options, expectations about the future, and number of sellers. As in the case of demand, price is the only *determinant of the quantity supplied.*

Demand and supply together define a market. In the absence of one or the other, there is no market.

DIE ANOTHER DAY

Rated PG-13/2002/2hrs 12 min/Pierce Brosnan, Halle Berry
Directed by Lee Tamahori

James Bond (Pierce Brosnan) has a series of interwoven adventures across the globe. At first, he impersonates an arms dealer who seeks to buy military equipment with diamonds in the demilitarized zone between North Korea and South Korea. He gets caught and ends up in prison where he waits for his government to organize a prisoner exchange. Once free, he seeks revenge, a process that takes him on an adventure to Cuba. There he meets Jinx (Halle Berry), and at first does not know what she is doing and whose side she is on. Meanwhile, the name of the billionaire Gustav Graves keeps cropping up. It turns out he is building a space mirror that beams solar light and heat using diamonds. Bond does not trust him and, while investigating his activities, ends up in Iceland where he finds Jinx is doing the same.

Economic Concepts in *Die Another Day*

Scene 3 (0:00–2:06)/ Minutes 4:28–6:34

James Bond, an agent of the British Secret Intelligence Service, is trying to gather information on North Korea, an enemy country. He has disguised himself as an illegal arms trader in order to gain access to the North Korean leaders. He has traveled to the demilitarized zone between North and South Korea where he has an appointment with Colonel Moon, a representative of the North Korean army.

Suave and self-assured, James Bond descends from a helicopter. He peers through his dark sunglasses at the desolate landscape peppered with busy men in military fatigues. Moon's assistant Zao is waiting impatiently.

Bond has come to North Korea ostensibly to buy weapons. Specifically, he is interested in buying hovercrafts, rocket-propelled grenades (RPGs), automatic weapons, and ammunition. He has a demand for them, and Moon has a supply of them. Given that they each demand what the other can supply, Bond and Moon have come together to trade. Their individual demand and supply is a tiny part of the total market for weapons.

Payment for the weapons will not be made with money but rather with diamonds. The price of the weapons package, in diamonds, has been prearranged. Bond has the agreed upon quantity of diamonds in his briefcase—that is his supply. In the absence of such an agreement, it is likely that the law of demand and the law of supply would be in effect during on-the-spot negotiations. In other words, if the price of weapons were to go up, Bond would demand less of them; if the price of diamonds were to go up, Bond would try to supply more of them.

While Zao passes Bond's diamonds to a specialist for evaluation, Bond's gaze falls on Moon's collection of luxury automobiles just off to the right. A crew of cleaners is polishing a Porsche and a Ferrari. Bond asks Moon if he will use the new diamonds to buy more such cars (in other words, will there be an increased demand for luxury cars?). Moon says no, he has other bigger plans for the stones. His enigmatic response does not imply that automobiles are inferior goods (they are normal goods, like hovercrafts and diamonds) but rather, for whatever reasons, his tastes have changed.

The diamonds have been inspected and are found to be of the highest quality. Their sparkle and purity does not change the fact that they are illegal and therefore should not be traded. As Bond states, they are the so-called blood diamonds, mined in conflict areas such as Sierra Leone and Angola where diamond revenues fuel rebel groups and perpetuate civil wars. The United Nations imposed restrictions in trade of such diamonds in 2000, so the suppliers have to turn to illegal markets to sell them. That means that the supplier will fetch a lower price than if the diamonds were legal since buyers are taking a risk and have to be compensated for that risk. Similarly, when Bond, a middleman in the diamond trade, sells illegal diamonds to Moon, he fetches a higher price than he would for legal diamonds since he bears a huge risk that could result in penalties and jail. In the film scene, Bond tells Moon how much his African Ministry friends are glad that someone is willing to trade in conflict diamonds, despite the embargo.

Then the hovercrafts are brought out for Bond's inspection. Moon points out an additional feature that distinguishes them from others: they float over mines. Since mines detonate under physical pressure, this floating feature was introduced in order to easily hide weapons in the demilitarized zone, where the United States left one million mines after the Korean War. The point of the American action was to ensure the demilitarized zone remained demilitarized. This plan clearly failed since North Korea nevertheless managed to hide weapons there by producing floating hovercrafts that do not detonate under pressure. This feature boosts the demand for North Korean hovercrafts and pushes their price above similar vehicles that do not float.

Discussion Questions

1. Many young women look forward to getting a diamond engagement ring. Few wonder about the source of the diamond. Yet many diamonds sold in the West are blood diamonds. Comment: As long as there is Western demand for diamonds, conflict zones will supply them.
2. James Bond refers to the United Nations embargo on diamonds that is meant to disrupt the diamond market. Is the purpose of an embargo to stem supply or demand of a good? Who is breaking the law by trading in diamonds—James Bond who supplies them or General Moon who demands them?
3. James Bond has traveled to an enemy country because he ostensibly has a demand for weapons. In reality, given his role in the British Secret Service, he has a demand for something else. What is it?

THE SNEETCHES

By Dr. Seuss
New York: Random House, 1989

There are Sneetches with a star on their bellies and Sneetches without. The Star-Bellied Sneetches consider themselves superior and won't have anything to do with the Plain-Belly ones. When Sylvester McMonkey McBean comes along touting his star-making business, the division between the

Sneetches is turned upside down. The Plain-Belly Sneetches line up to have their bellies starred so as to be part of the in crowd. But the Star-Belly Sneetches do not want to look like these new imposters so they hire Mr. McBean to remove their stars. A domino effect ensues as all the Sneetches in town begin replacing and removing stars from their bellies until one day they call a truce. They decide to stop viewing belly stars as a mark that distinguishes one Sneetch from another.

Economic Concepts in *The Sneetches*

pp. 8–9

Plain-Belly Sneetches are depressed because the Star-Belly Sneetches had a frankfurter roast on the beach and would not allow them to join in on the fun. They were not permitted to participate because even though they have the same bizarre potbellies, bright yellow skin, and elongated necks, the Plain-Belly Sneetches do not have stars on their bellies.

As they lie around moping and feeling sorry for themselves, a strange man shows up driving an even stranger car. He introduces himself, "My name is Sylvester McMonkey McBean," and then explains that he has heard of their troubles and has come to help out. He is selling a service: stamping stars on bellies. He has recognized that there is a demand for such a service, namely that Sneetches will pay money to become star-bellied, and he is responding to that demand by supplying this innovative service. He says, "I've come here to help you. I have what you need."

Mr. McBean is the first provider of such a service. He is the first to recognize the latent desire of the Plain-Bellied Sneetches to become star-bellied. They don't have a demand for a star-making service because it never occurrs to them that such a service might exist. Once they learn about it, they have a demand. Therefore one could say that Mr. McBean creates the demand for his service simply by offering it on the market.

In light of convincing information about this new service, the Plain-Belly Sneetches get in line to have their bellies stamped with a star. Their aggregated demand represents the market demand. It is abundant, and Mr. McBean knows it. Indeed, it is unlikely he would have driven his star-stamping car all the way to the Sneetches' beach for just one Sneetch's demand for a star.

When Mr. McBean realizes just how much Sneetches are willing to pay for a star (or rather, for becoming one of the popular starred Sneetches), he becomes motivated to supply more of his product. His behavior illustrates the law of supply as he takes his innovative machine over to a new group of consumers, the Star-Belly Sneetches, suggesting they should remove the stars from their bellies (and thus differentiate themselves from the imposter starred Sneetches to whom he has just sold his services). By convincing this new group of Sneetches to purchase his product, Mr. McBean ingeniously expands the market for his service.

Incidentally, Mr. McBean is a savvy businessman. When first introducing his service, he tells the Plain-Belly Sneetches, "My prices are low. And I work at great speed. And my work is one hundred per cent guaranteed!" Even though he is the only supplier of his product, McBean drums up demand by assuring potential customers that the purchase of his service will not make a big dent in their wallets. The fact that he works fast is also meant to stimulate demand by assuring buyers that the star stamping will not take up too much of their time (McBean is considerate of the opportunity cost of their time). Finally, by guaranteeing his work, Mr. McBean implies that he will remove it for free if the buyers are not satisfied. Low prices, speed of execution, and free removal all serve to induce the Sneetches to get in line for a star tattoo.

Discussion Questions

1. When you are disappointed with your iPod from 2004 and desire your friend's 2008 model, is your demand similar to that of a Plain-belly Sneetch? Explain, keeping in mind the upcoming 2009 model.
2. Mr. McBean wouldn't have driven his star-making car all the way to the Sneetches' beach just to satisfy one Sneetch's demand for a star. He must have expected a large market demand for his service. Can you think of any products that are produced for one buyer only? What about services?
3. A local shop, *Tattoos By Tommy,* gives student discounts for body tattoos. Across the street, a local dermatologist uses lasers to remove tattoos and advertises special rates for students. Using the law of demand, explain what Tommy and the dermatologist are trying to achieve.

Chapter 5

Specialization

Film: *GONE WITH THE WIND*
Fiction: *SNOW WHITE AND THE SEVEN DWARFS*

KEY ECONOMIC CONCEPTS

Modern societies are not *self-sufficient*. Their households and firms do not produce everything they need or want. Instead, they produce some goods and services while trading in the marketplace for others. For example, most people do not grow their own food, or build their own houses, or fix their own cars, or sew their own clothes. They identify what they are most proficient in, and then they focus on producing that or, as economists say, they specialize in that production. Through such *specialization*, they become farmers, architects, mechanics, and tailors.

Once they have specialized, they then sell their output to others who have different specializations. With their earnings, they purchase goods and services produced by others. In other words, everyone exchanges, and in the process, everyone becomes better off (gains from trade are discussed in chapter 6).

Through specialization, *division of labor* is established that indicates what specialized goods and services each individual offers for exchange.

What is the basis for such division of labor? In other words, how do people (firms or countries) decide on their specializations? According to *absolute advantage*, an individual specializes in the production of the good he can make more of, using the same resources as his competitors. Alternatively, according to *comparative advantage*, an individual should specialize in the production of the good she can produce at a lower opportunity cost than her competitors.

Specialization is dynamic. When conditions change, people, firms, and countries adapt by changing their specializations.

GONE WITH THE WIND

Rated G/1939/3hrs 53 min/Clark Gable, Vivien Leigh
Directed by Victor Fleming
Winner of eight Academy Awards, including Best Picture, Director, Actress

This is a classic—one of the most watched films of all time. It is the story of a southern plantation-owning family, during the Civil War. The main character is Scarlett O'Hara (Vivien Leigh), a wealthy and fickle young woman who grows up to successfully meet all of life's challenges. While many men loved her, she loved and pursued only Ashley, even after his marriage to her friend. When the Civil War breaks out, Scarlett's family loses their estate, Tara, and becomes poor and scattered. Scarlett is strong and picks up the pieces. She marries Rhett Butler (Clark Gable), a wealthy businessman, but the marriage is replete with misunderstandings and miscommunications; it ultimately fails. Throughout, Scarlett's resilience enables her to survive all the pain that has come her way.

Economic Concepts in *Gone With the Wind*

Scene 10 (0:00–1:36)/ Minutes 25:44–27:20

Before the Civil War, wealthy southern families frequently had parties on their plantations that lasted over the course of an entire day. Scarlett and her family are guests at one such party at the Hamilton Estate in Georgia. As is the custom, after an opulent midday meal the women retreat to the bedrooms for an afternoon nap while the men congregate in the shaded living rooms for cigars, brandy, and conversation about world events.

Scarlett O'Hara is different from other young women and resents being forced to rest. While her peers sleep, she sneaks out and makes her way down the grandiose staircase. With every step, she hears more of the heated political arguments taking place in the men's quarters. She listens, fascinated, all the while maneuvering her puffy dress to hide from sight.

The discussion focuses on the upcoming Civil War. Someone introduces Mr. Butler, a gentleman who has spent time in the North, and asks his opinion on the economic and political situation. Rhett Butler explains that the division of labor across the united American colonies gives an advantage to the North in the upcoming war. This is because all economic activity needed for the war effort takes place in the North. Yankees, Butler claims, have factories, shipyards, coal mines, and an impressive fleet. They have specialized in the production of these strategic industries that directly aid in the war effort. Simultaneously, they have also diversified their economy to produce a broad range of supporting goods (such as food) that indirectly help them wage war.

By contrast, Butler adds, the South has been producing cotton and an overabundance of gentlemen plantation owners, neither of which will be useful in the war effort. In fact, there is not a single cannon factory in the South. That means Georgians have to import from the North the very goods that they need to fight the North.

This division of labor in pre-Civil War American society evolved because the South had a comparative advantage in the production of cotton while the North had an advantage in the production of manufactured goods. According to Butler, slavery in the South had a role in determining this division of labor. Indeed, slavery gave the South a comparative advantage in the production of cotton because it provided free work in an industry that was highly labor-intensive and required an abundance of workers. The North, not having slaves, tended to adopt production techniques that relied less on labor and more on machinery. Such manufacturing techniques are more modern, efficient, and capable of large output increases.

The cigar-puffing plantation owners are crowding around Butler, listening attentively as he speaks. As further evidence of the South's precarious position, Butler says, the North can easily close off Georgia's ports as Yankees have specialized in ship production and have amassed a huge fleet. By closing off the ports, the North can block all trade, thereby preventing Georgia from selling its output (cotton) and earning income needed for the war. In addition, blocked ports also prevent the state from purchasing goods, including food to feed its population as well as ammunition to fight the war.

While the scenario described by Butler is common during wartime, the southern gentlemen seem too remote from reality to grasp it. Butler walks away in frustration.

Discussion Questions

1. The South specialized in cotton production while the North specialized in manufacturing. Although economically less developed, the South wanted to secede from the Union, believing its economy could survive without the North. If the South had succeeded in seceding, how would its economy have adjusted to the loss of manufacturing from the North? In

other words, how would it have satisfied the demand for the goods previously supplied by the North?

2. What happened to the South's comparative advantage in the production of cotton after the abolition of slavery?

3. In *Gone With the Wind*, the division of labor between the North and the South is explained in detail while the division of labor between men and women is not addressed. The fact that women rest after lunch while men congregate to discuss politics gives a hint of the differing roles men and women in wealthy plantation households played. Do you think a similar division of labor between genders also existed among the slave populations that worked on the plantations? Why or why not?

SNOW WHITE AND THE SEVEN DWARFS

By Jacob and Wilhelm Grimm
The Complete Grimm's Fairy Tales
New York: Pantheon Books, 1972

In a kingdom, long ago, an evil Queen looked at herself in the mirror every day and asked, "Mirror, mirror on the wall, who is the fairest of us all?" For years the mirror responded that she was the one until one day, the mirror said it was Snow White, her stepdaughter, who was prettier. The Queen could not bear the competition. She ordered one of the palace hunters to take the girl into the woods and kill her. The hunter, a kind man, could not bring himself to commit such an act and left the poor girl in the forest unharmed. Snow White spent a few scary days in the forest, meandering, until she came across the house of the Seven Dwarfs. They happily took her in and she lived a peaceful life with them until, one day, the Queen showed up. She had been told by the mirror that Snow White was still the fairest in the land so she came, with a poisoned apple, to finish the job the hunter left undone. However, all ends happily as the evil Queen has an accident and Snow White marries a handsome prince and lives happily ever after.

Economic Concepts in *Snow White and the Seven Dwarfs*

p. 251

After days of wandering through dense forests and scratching her delicate arms on protruding twigs, Snow White comes upon a quaint little house with colorful window shutters. She approaches the door, too exhausted to be cautious. When no one answers her knocks, she bravely turns the knob and enters. There are seven identical beds, chairs, and table settings. It is the beds that draw her in and she collapses across them, falling into a deep slumber.

Snow White wakes up to find seven dwarfs at her bedside. When she tells them her sad tale, namely that her stepmother tried to have her killed, the dwarfs are overcome with compassion and promptly make a suggestion. She can stay and live with them, but it involves a trade. They will give her room and board and in exchange, she needs to take care of their home. In other words, she must cook their meals, make the beds, wash their laundry, mend their clothes, and generally keep their home neat and clean. If she does all that, they say, she will "want for nothing."

And so a trade is negotiated, and Snow White accepts the dwarfs' offer. Each side is better off: she gets a place to live that is safe from her stepmother while they get housekeeping services. Gains from trade are achieved by everyone and are based on the specialization each party brings to the negotiating table. Snow White specializes in housekeeping—that is an activity she knows how to perform as her stepmother had required similar work of her. The dwarfs specialize in mining and are less efficient in household activities. With Snow White performing those household chores, the dwarfs can now spend more time working on what they do best, mining for gold and copper. Since the dwarfs are older and stronger and more experienced, it is possible that they have an absolute advantage over Snow White in both the production of housework as well as mined resources. However, trade between the two parties will nevertheless take place because, while they have a comparative advantage in the extraction of copper and gold, Snow White has a comparative advantage in the production of housework.

Discussion Questions

1. What is the division of labor in your household? On what basis are chores divided between you and the people with whom you share a home?

2. If Snow White had a degree in accounting, how might that have changed her arrangement with the dwarfs?

3. Dr. Brane is a neurosurgeon working long hours at the hospital. She hires a housekeeper to perform household chores, such as cooking and cleaning and driving the children's carpools. Explain the division of labor in the Brane household using the concepts of comparative advantage and opportunity cost.

Chapter 6

Gains From Exchange

Film: *TWINS*
Fiction: *ANIMAL FARM*

KEY ECONOMIC CONCEPTS

Trade in goods (and services and factors) occurs because it makes people better off. If people did not *gain from exchange,* there would be no *incentive to trade,* so trade would not take place. The gain is not necessarily measured in money as there are also *nonmonetary incentives* to trade. Irrespective of the form of the benefit, trading allows everyone to achieve a more desirable outcome.

Trade that involves exchange of one good (or service or factor) for another, in the absence of money, is called *barter*. Barter, however, is inefficient and time-consuming. For it to be successful, each trader has to have exactly what the other wants. Most trade is not barter but rather entails the exchange of a good for money. It involves buyers and sellers who voluntarily trade in order to benefit. It avoids the inefficiencies of barter.

Traders do not benefit equally. The benefit to buyers depends on their demand for a particular good and the price at which they buy it. Economists use the concept of *consumer surplus* to measure the benefit they derive. Consumer surplus is the difference between the amount an individual is willing to pay for a good and the amount actually paid for it. For example: Ms. Smith goes to Macy's expecting to pay $100 for a coat but gets the coat she wants for $60. Her consumer surplus is $40.

A similar concept exists to explain the benefit of trade to suppliers. *Producer surplus* is the difference between the lowest price of a good at which suppliers are willing to supply it and the actual price that they receive when they sell it. For example, Acme Water Shop is willing to supply bottled water for 99¢ but actually sells it for $1.29. The producer surplus is 30¢.

Sometimes trade cannot take place freely. Governments introduce restrictions and regulations that dictate the quantity of a good that can be sold and the circumstances under which trade can occur. Such *barriers to trade* limit the overall gains from exchange that are experienced by the traders.

When trade occurs, *transaction costs* are incurred. These are the costs of trading that are in addition to the price of the goods being traded. They include, for example, travel to the place of trade, import or export duties, and currency conversion fees.

TWINS

Rated PG/1988/107 min//Danny DeVito, Arnold Schwarzenegger
Directed by Ivan Reitman

In a genetics lab, an experiment produces twin boys that are very different from birth. The handsome, strong one is retained for further experimentation while the ugly weakling is given up for adoption. Julius (Arnold Schwarzenegger) grows up to be highly educated, strong in body and spirit, and extremely handsome. By contrast, Vincent (Danny DeVito) grows up in an orphanage and becomes a grouchy thief. He is neither bright nor attractive. When Julius learns that he has a twin, he embarks upon a journey to find him. Together they have some misadventures as Julius tries to wean Vincent from crime and convince him that they are in fact twins. His efforts come to a head when Vincent becomes embroiled in criminal activity that could net him $5 million but might also cost him his life.

Economic Concepts in *Twins*

Scene 8 (3:38–5:43)/ Minutes 44:40–46:46

Vincent has perfected a lucrative scam. With the cooperation of the parking attendant at a Los Angeles garage, he steals automobiles with high resale value and then sells them to a local criminal. The attendant receives a cut, and Vincent pockets several thousand dollars per car. Vincent never expects to net a huge sale but that does not bother him—his income is more or less steady and he is not a man with large expectations. He is generally content with his life. All that changes the day he steals the wrong car.

That wrong car is a sparkling clean Cadillac parked on an upper floor. After first fiddling with its lock and then fiddling with the wires, Vincent drives out of the garage humming happily. Seeking entertainment, he explores the music possibilities. There is a tape in the tape deck, so he listens, expecting to sing along to a popular tune. Instead, a stern man's voice fills the car. The voice gives instructions as to where to deliver "the goods." Vincent assumes the tape refers to the Cadillac and figures he might get a better price by calling the number on the tape than by peddling it through his usual connection.

He drives home and makes the call. Emboldened by his seemingly good luck, Vincent decides to ask for an outrageous sum for the delivery of the car: $20,000. Shortly into the conversation with a burly sounding Texan, Vincent realizes that he will be paid $5 million upon delivery. Five million dollars! Vincent has no idea that the Cadillac contains a rocket launcher in the trunk.

Both Vincent and the Texan will benefit from the trade. Vincent will be better off because he will get paid for his service (delivery) and for the product he will deliver (a rocket launcher). The Texan will be made better off because he will acquire a good that is difficult to obtain and for which he has a strong demand.

Vincent is willing to deliver the Cadillac for $20,000 yet he will receive $5 million. That translates into a producer surplus of $4,980,000.00. Clearly he will benefit from the trade.

The Texan is willing to pay such a high price because there are huge barriers to trade in rocket launchers. Those barriers exist because the supply of rocket launchers is limited, given huge government regulation of the industry. Outside legitimate channels, trading rocket launchers is illegal as it inevitably serves illicit purposes. Indeed, such illegal sales are usually associated with rogue states and terrorist activity. As a result, transaction costs are very high in order to compensate for the risk of transporting stolen merchandise and concealing its identity.

Such trade is beyond the expertise of Vincent who is, after all, just a petty thief. Nevertheless, he pursues it with a vengeance and sets out on a long road trip to make the delivery. His efforts are complicated by Julius, his do-good twin who keeps trying to make him honest. Julius comes along for the ride, as do Vincent's girlfriend and her sister.

Julius does not understand that even if Vincent decides to turn over a new leaf and resist the temptation to pocket $5 million, he cannot stop. He has compelling nonmonetary incentives to engage in the trade with the Texan because by now the bad guys—the ones for whom the loaded Cadillac was originally intended—know his identity and are on his trail.

Discussion Questions

1. The stolen car industry thrives in the United States. Surprisingly, it is the cheaper cars (such as Hondas) that are stolen more frequently than the expensive ones (such as Porsches). Explain this phenomenon using the concept of barriers to trade.
2. What are the transaction costs that Vincent will incur while making his delivery? Do these costs include the opportunity cost of Vincent's time?
3. Think of the last few consumer goods you bought. Did you actually pay less for any of them than you would have? Explain your purchase in terms of consumer surplus.

ANIMAL FARM

By George Orwell
New York: Signet, 1996

An incompetent farmer owns Manor Farm. He is too drunk to effectively manage his holdings so one day the animals, tired of his mismanagement, revolt and run him off the farm. They take over the land and the house and try to set up a model community in which there will be equality and abundance for all animals. They call it Animal Farm. Two pigs, Napoleon and Snowball, emerge as leaders. But there is not enough space at the top for two pigs so Napoleon declares Snowball to be a traitor and runs him off the farm. The animals believe, at first, that they can be self-sufficient but later come to see that economic interaction with neighboring farms is necessary. Over time, they also come to see that differences between animals are inevitable and some become more "equal" than others. Napoleon becomes a dictator, and the animals are no better off than they had been under the control of humans.

Economic Concepts in *Animal Farm*

pp. 62–63

The animals have taken over the farm. They are delirious with excitement, enjoying their first experience as owners and managers of all farm resources and activities. Each horse, cow, chicken, and goat now walks with a quickened gait and holds his or her head up higher than before. Finally there are no more humans to kick them around and treat them as . . . well, as animals. They work very hard, each striving to contribute as much as possible to the farm, and therefore, to the common good.

It turns out, however, that even if they are more efficient than humans in numerous tasks (such as weeding), they still do not produce enough eggs, wheat, and other farm goods. They cannot produce enough output because they do not have enough inputs (such as paraffin oil, nails, string, or iron for horses' shoes) that enable them to produce more. Over time, the situation gets worse as the animals begin to require seeds, artificial manure, and machinery in order to continue producing.

And so, with great frustration and sorrow, the animals realize that they are not as self-sufficient as they previously thought. They need to trade in several markets outside of their farm, with the very humans that they so despise. As a result, Napoleon, the leader of Animal Farm, introduces a new policy for the farm community: farm production will henceforth be focused on goods for sale, not for animal consumption. On the farm, everyone will have to tighten their belts and put all their energies into producing goods to sell off the farm.

Napoleon assures his subjects that this trade is in the best interest of all farm animals as the income earned through exchange will be used to purchase nails and machinery, which are the much-needed inputs into farm production. By marketing output to neighbors, in exchange for money, Napoleon is showing he is motivated by monetary incentives.

The new policy specifically notes which crops must now be produced for sale: one stack of hay, a part of the current year's wheat crop, and eggs. These are chosen because the demand for them is constant in the neighboring town of Willingdon. It follows that where there is demand, there will be income for the supplier. Napoleon is counting on that income.

Although Napoleon is a pig, he is also a shrewd businessman. He knows that trade entails transaction costs, such as transportation of goods to the market, that must be subtracted from the earnings. He is also aware of the opportunity costs incurred by the animals that are not actively involved in farm production while they are driving the transport truck.

Finally, Napoleon undoubtedly also considers the barriers to trade that Animal Farm sellers might encounter when they take their goods to Willingdon's markets. These include inclement weather that will prevent timely transport, as well as resistance by humans to trading with animals that they consider inferior.

Discussion Questions

1. Animal Farm may be a fantasy, but it is fact that animals and humans have interacted throughout history. Some animals become pets and live with humans. Use the concept of gains from exchange to explain the relationship between pets and their owners.

2. Napoleon wants to sell eggs and hay in exchange for money. Why doesn't he barter those goods for seeds and machinery?

3. Several centuries ago, family farms were largely self-sufficient entities that produced what they consumed and consumed what they produced. Over time, specialized farms (that produce a limited number of products) became the norm. How did these modern farms satisfy their consumptive needs? Explain using key concepts.

Chapter 7

Prices

Film: *PIRATES OF THE CARIBBEAN: THE CURSE OF THE BLACK PEARL*
Fiction: *OLIVER TWIST*

KEY ECONOMIC CONCEPTS

When the quantity demanded of a good is equal to the quantity supplied, the market is in *equilibrium*. The price at which this equilibrium occurs is the *market price*. If this price is determined with no interference from the government, then it is a free market price.

Markets are usually not in equilibrium. Sometimes there is a *shortage*, namely a situation in which quantity demanded exceeds quantity supplied and there is not enough to satisfy everyone's wishes to buy. Alternatively there might be a *surplus*, which occurs when the quantity demanded is lower than the quantity supplied. In this case, there is an overflow of goods that no one wants to buy.

In either of these two *disequilibrium* conditions, there is pressure on prices to rise or fall until the equilibrium price is reached. At that time, the shortage or surplus is eliminated.

Prices are not always given in terms of dollars (or any currency). Sometimes they are given in terms of another good (that is, the price of a chicken in tomatoes). These are *nonmonetary prices*.

PIRATES OF THE CARIBBEAN: THE CURSE OF THE BLACK PEARL

Rated PG-13/2003/2hr 23 min/Johnny Depp, Orlando Bloom, Keira Knightley
Directed by Gore Verbinski

Elizabeth Swann (Keira Knightley) possesses a gold necklace. While she loves to wear it, the pirates of the Black Pearl need it in order to lift a curse made on them when they stole some Aztec gold years before. In order to obtain the necklace, the pirates attack Port Royal where Elizabeth lives with her father, Governor Weatherby Swann (Jonathan Pryce), and kidnap her. Three men try to rescue her: Norrington (Jack Davenport), who wants to marry her; William Turner (Orlando Bloom) whom Elizabeth secretly loves; and Captain Jack Sparrow (Johnny Depp), a pirate with a sense of justice. Captain Sparrow has ulterior motives in his rescue mission. He was treated badly by Barbossa (Geoffrey Rush), the captain of the Black Pearl, and he seeks revenge. In this film, Elizabeth and her three rescuers have numerous adventures as they try to save their lives.

Economic Concepts in *The Pirates of the Caribbean*

Scene 2 (1:06–1:46)/ Minutes 9:58–10:38

Captain Sparrow arrives in Port Royal on a bright sunny day. He pulls up to the dock in a small boat and descends onto land with agility. Despite his disheveled hair, his raggedy clothing, and a long dangling earring, he evokes no interest among the townsfolk. A nearby fisherman is repairing his fishing net while a uniformed navy sergeant is staring into the horizon. Just as Sparrow is about to sigh with relief that no one has yelled out, "A pirate!" the pier guard stops him. With an imposing hat and black cloak befitting the times, the guard respectfully reminds this obviously first-time visitor to Port Royal that he must pay a fee in order to dock his boat.

On that particular sunny day, the equilibrium price of docking is one shilling. It is the price at which the quantity of docking places demanded is equal to the number of docking spaces available. It is likely that the fee for docking is set by the guard in response to daily changing conditions. If many boats seek to dock, such as when the annual fencing competition draws residents from adjoining islands, then the guard raises the price. Similarly, when the weather is foul, there is little nautical traffic so the demand for docking spaces is low. At such times, the guard drops the price. Being on the ground, the guard has the best overview of changing demand and supply conditions. By empowering him to determine the equilibrium price of docking, shortages and surpluses are avoided.

An alternative way of arriving at the price of docking is for Governor Swann to set it. Being a conscientious man, the governor is likely to put a lot of care into determining the most appropriate price. He is likely to study demand and supply patterns over the past few years and collect information about their determinants. Still, the price he arrives at will not be immune to shortages and surpluses. It would have all the problems associated with prices in command economies, while empowering the guard to set prices that would have the advantages of market prices.

In addition to the one shilling fee, there is one other price under discussion in the docking scene of *Pirates of the Caribbean*. When the guard asks Sparrow for money, he wants something else as well. He wants Sparrow's name so as to make note of it in his big black ledger. In order to keep records of port activity, the names of all visitors must be recorded in ink by the guard. It is the law, and to comply, the guard demands to know Sparrow's name. Sparrow withholds the supply of that information. He fears his name will be recognized. Once his identity is made public, the time before he hangs on the central square for piracy is not distant. Therefore, Sparrow is willing to pay money not to reveal his name. Sparrow offers to buy the guard's cooperation. He wants him to withhold his name from the book of visitors. Placing three coins on the guard's ledger, Sparrow says, "What do you say to three shillings, and we forget the name?"

Sparrow hesitated for a moment, wondering if his offer price was in fact the equilibrium price. When the guard closed the ledger, muttered, "Welcome to Port Royal," and looked away, Sparrow knew he was in the clear. This was an indication that the *de facto* price negotiations had been concluded, that his offer price was just right, or possibly even higher than the guard expected. Sparrow made his way down the pier with a springy gait, unaware of the many adventures that awaited him.

Film watchers probably wonder why Sparrow didn't simply provide a fake name. Had he called himself Smith or Jones, his price for parking would have been only one shilling rather than the three shillings he ended up paying. But that would have involved lying about his name, which Sparrow was unwilling to do.

Discussion Questions

1. Comment: If the guard had refused the three shillings, Captain Sparrow should simply have offered more. After all, everybody has a price.

2. Imagine: In honor of the expected upcoming nuptials between Elizabeth and Norrington, Governor Swann makes some big investments in Port Royal. He builds a new church, repaves the town square, and extends the dock all the way to the next cove. He is, after all, expecting many

guests to arrive by ship for his daughter's wedding. What will happen to the price of docking in Port Royal?

3. Parking garages in American cities have set prices, and customers do not negotiate with the parking attendant. Explain why the garages sometimes make an exception and charge a flat fee for parking after 6 p.m. on weekends.

OLIVER TWIST

By Charles Dickens
New York: Random House, 2001

This story of the difficult life of Oliver Twist, an orphan living in England in the 1800s, begins in his foster home just outside of London. Oliver is always hungry, and his growth is stunted because the woman paid by the City Council to take care of him spends his food money on herself. Oliver's hunger persists when he is moved to an orphanage and even later, when he becomes an apprentice chimney sweep. It seems that Oliver cannot avoid evil, especially when he ends up in London, forced to work as a pickpocket for the criminal Fagan. His luck seems to turn when the generous Mr. Brownlow takes Oliver in and provides him with ample food, education, and affection. Oliver thrives but is soon kidnapped by criminals and forced to engage in more illegal activities. A complicated story ensues.

Economic Concepts in *Oliver Twist*

pp. 19–20

After Oliver has the audacity to ask for more food at the orphanage, the Parish Board decides it is time to get rid of him. He has become too expensive to maintain, and his demands for extra nourishment are riling up the other boys, leading them to also demand more.

The Parish Board posts a sign in town, offering Oliver up as an apprentice worker. As such, Oliver would perform tasks for his boss in exchange for room and board. He would receive no cash income. Learning a trade was considered sufficient payment during the 1800s in England. To entice someone to take Oliver, the Parish Board offers to pay five British pounds, supposedly to cover initial expenses until the boy acquires sufficient skills to begin paying his keep. In reality, the Board is offering a reward of five pounds to whomever takes Oliver off their hands. This is the price at which Oliver is supplied to the apprentice market.

Gamfield runs a chimney-cleaning service and needs a new apprentice, a young boy who will perform the unpleasant task of climbing into tight chimney spaces. Gamfield sees the posted signs about Oliver and, given his demand for such a boy, makes his way to the parish to make a deal. However, as soon as he proposes the exchange at the aforementioned price, the greedy Parish Board members see an opportunity to save money. They reduce the reward.

Negotiations begin to find a new equilibrium price. The Board uses two points to argue that they should pack Oliver off for less than five pounds. First they claim that Oliver will not cost Gamfield much in maintenance since he eats very little. In fact, they proudly state that Oliver has not been well fed since he was born. They even suggest that Gamfield should control Oliver's food portions so as to stunt his growth, ensuring he remains small and slender, just right for the tight chimney passages.

The Board's second argument is intended to lower Gamfield's negotiating power by reminding him of his bad reputation. Everyone knows that Gamfield is a vicious owner who mistreats his apprentices, they say. Indeed, three or four boys in his care have already died, smothered in chimneys. By feigning concern for Oliver's safety and attacking Gamfield's risky business, the Board members hope to catch him off guard when they offer a lower reward.

Their new offer is three pounds and fifty pence. Gamfield holds out for four pounds. They finally agree to stop haggling and split the difference because each side has become nervous. The Board feared Gamfield would walk away (together with his demand for a chimney sweep) while Gamfield feared the Board would change its mind (withhold supply).

The fact that the orphanage offers Oliver up for apprenticeship indicates a surplus of boys like him. It also explains why the final equilibrium price is relatively low. Had there been fewer orphan boys, people like Gamfield would have had to pay much more for chimney sweeps.

In considering the Board's supply price for Oliver, Gamfield makes his own calculations. He evaluates Oliver's probable life expectancy as a chimney sweep—most boys do not live very long as the smut in their lungs kills them or an accidental fall breaks their bones. Longevity calculations feature prominently in Gamfield's thinking about the maximum price he would pay to get Oliver as an apprentice—he assumes Oliver won't be around long enough to work off a large purchase price. In this way, expectations about the future have an effect on the price Gamfield is willing to pay.

Discussion Questions

1. The Parish Board decided to get rid of Oliver because his appetite had become too large. Imagine if instead of offering him into apprenticeship, the orphanage had put him to work in a garden where he could

grow food for himself and the other boys. What effect would that have had on supply, demand, and equilibrium prices in the local food market?

2. Americans adopted some twenty-one thousand children from foreign orphanages in 2006. Explain that in terms of shortage, surplus, and equilibrium in the U.S. market for adoptable children.

3. If Oliver had eaten a lot and been overweight, Gamfield would not have wanted him as a chimney sweep. Can you think of jobs in contemporary society in which body weight or size is either an advantage or a disadvantage in determining the demand (and price) of labor?

II

MICROECONOMIC TOPICS

Chapter 8

Price Elasticity

Film: *MICHAEL CLAYTON*
Fiction: *TO HAVE AND HAVE NOT*

KEY ECONOMIC CONCEPTS

According to the law of demand, when the price of a good goes up, the quantity demanded by consumers will go down. By how much will demand decrease? In other words, how sensitive are consumers to price changes? Economists refer to the *price elasticity of demand* to answer that question.

Price elasticity of demand for any good or service is found by dividing the percent change in the quantity demanded by the percent change in price. High price elasticity of demand indicates great consumer sensitivity and is common among most goods and services, such as new cars and vacations. Low price elasticity of demand tends to be more common with *necessities* (that take up a small portion of one's budget, such as electricity and coffee) and high-end luxury items. Additional determinants of elasticity include, among others, the *share of the good in a consumer's budget* and the *availability of substitutes*.

Elasticity is a crucial measure as it allows producers to consider if raising prices is worth it. In other words, if they raise prices, they might lose so many customers (as per the law of demand) that they might have been better off before when the prices were lower. This line of thought involves considering the *total revenue* earned by the seller, as measured by the number of goods sold by their price. When demand is *inelastic* (or low), then a price increase will result in an increase in revenue. When demand is *elastic* (or high), a price increase will result in a decrease in revenue.

Elasticity estimates are the basis for *price discrimination*, namely when sellers charge different consumers differing prices. They do that since people do not all have the same elasticities and so are willing to pay different prices for the same good. For example, business travelers and leisure travelers are willing to pay different amounts for airline travel because the former have an inelastic demand while the latter's is elastic.

The concept of elasticity is also used to gauge how sensitive suppliers are to price changes (the *price elasticity of supply*) as well as how responsive buyers are to changes in their income (the *income elasticity of demand*).

MICHAEL CLAYTON

Rated R/2007/1hr 58min/George Clooney, Tom Wilkinson, Tilda Swinton
Directed by Tony Gilroy
Winner of Academy Award for Best Supporting Actress

Attorney Michael Clayton (George Clooney) is Mr. Fix-It at a New York law firm where he has years of experience in taking care of messy problems. He does not like his work but given his debt, gambling, and alcohol problems, Clayton has no alternatives. When one of the firm's partners, Arthur Edens (Tom Wilkinson) seemingly has a nervous breakdown in the middle of a huge case, Clayton comes to his friend's rescue. The case in question involves a class action suit against U-North, a major agrochemicals company. In his efforts to fix the problem, Clayton has several unpleasant encounters with U-North's general counsel Karen Crowder (Tilda Swinton). Events spin out of control as people die and Clayton's car blows up, all in pursuit of corporate interests.

Economic Concepts in *Michael Clayton*

Scene 25 (1:30–3:31)/ Minutes 1:45–1:49; (NOTE: this scene contains vulgar language.)
Scene 26 (0:00–4:20)/ Minutes 1:52–1:08

Arthur Edens has spent the last six years preparing the defense for U-North in a billion-dollar class action lawsuit. Recently he has come to believe that the plaintiff is right. He has found evidence that U-North is in fact using cancer-causing toxic chemicals in its pesticides and, even more damaging, that the company leadership knew and did not pull the products off the market. This information was embedded in an internal U-North memorandum that Edens obtained.

U-North litigator Crowder learns that Edens has turned and is now building a case against his own client, namely her company. She also finds that he has the condemning memo and has made one thousand copies that he plans to distribute publicly. She uses all means at her disposal to silence him, including intimidation, phone tapping, and ultimately murder.

A single riveting scene of *Michael Clayton* contains two illustrations of price elasticity. Crowder has just emerged from a hotel ballroom where the U-North Board of Directors has met to discuss her proposal to settle the pesticide case. As chief counsel, she had argued that a multimillion dollar settlement is in the best interest of the company because the tax write-off would pay for itself. Crowder did not share with the board members any information about Edens's activities or his photocopied memo. While the Board members deliberate, Crowder stands in a vast lobby outside the ballroom, breathless from her argument, confident her proposal will be accepted. Soon, she will be able to forget that she has broken the law. Soon her nightmare will be over.

But it's not over till it's over. Crowder spins around to find Michael Clayton leaning confidently against a paneled wall just behind her. In his hand is a rolled up memo, its red cover screaming out. It is unmistakable. Crowder's sensible heels seem to sprout roots into the plush pile of the wall-to-wall carpeting.

The ensuing conversation is about setting a price for the trade these two individuals can make. Clayton has the memo that incriminates U-North. He also has information about Crowder's illegal activities with respect to Arthur Edens. He is offering both for sale in a single package. He is the supplier.

Crowder has a demand for this package. She wants both the memo and assurance of his silence. She asks Clayton for his price.

When he says five million, she agrees ("Five million and I'll forget about Arthur's death"). Then he takes the price up to ten million, and she agrees again ("And another five million for the 468 people knocked off with your weed killer"). Her response indicates that her demand is price inelastic. In other words, she is so desperate to buy the memo together with his silence that she will accept either price.

Crowder's face becomes as pale as her suit jacket. She knows that ten million represents a huge proportion of her budget, but she feels she has no choice. The alternative is jail. She also knows that the package (memo plus silence) she seeks to buy has no substitutes. Even if there were another damaging memo making the rounds, it would not substitute for the one in Clayton's hand; even if someone else were privy to her wrongdoings, the information they have is not a substitute for the information Clayton has.

It turns out that Clayton is leading her on. He has no intention of selling the memo or his silence, not for five million and not for ten. He wants to be at peace with himself; he wants to avenge his friend's death. Ten million dollars will not get him that, so Clayton's supply is price inelastic.

Discussion Questions

1. Comment: Crowder's mistake was that she offered too little for Clayton's silence. She should have offered twenty million.
2. Edens made one thousand copies of the memorandum. Is Crowder's price elasticity of demand greater for one copy or for the whole box of one thousand copies?
3. Price elasticity of demand tends to be high for luxuries and low for necessities. How is Clayton's memo/silence both a luxury and a necessity for Crowder? If it is indeed both, then why do we say that her demand is price inelastic?

TO HAVE AND HAVE NOT

By Ernest Hemingway (winner of 1954 Nobel Prize in Literature)
New York: Scribner, 2003

This book takes place in Cuba during pre-Castro times. Harry Morgan is an American fisherman who makes an honest living renting out his boat to tourists. One of his clients cheats him out of his due: he leaves the island before paying for several days of fishing. Morgan is strapped. He can no longer afford to buy gasoline for his boat, nor can he make needed repairs. Although he is fundamentally an honest man, Morgan must resort to smuggling in order to survive. Then, as now, many Cubans try to emigrate to the United States. Morgan's route is between Havana and Key West, and his cargo all too often consists of emigrants. During his journeys, he encounters danger, corruption, wealth, love, and disappointment.

Economic Themes in *To Have and Have Not*

pp. 1–2

When Morgan is first offered money to smuggle people from Havana to Key West, he indignantly turns down the offer. He is, after all, an honorable fisherman, and even if he barely makes ends meet, he will not let himself be tempted into illegal activity.

The next day the offer is repeated. It happens when Morgan enters a café near the Havana dock for a well-deserved drink at the end of a strenuous workday. In the corner sits the man who just yesterday offered him the illegal job, together with two associates. They are finely dressed, clearly out of place among the ratty dockworkers, and have a slightly menacing demeanor. They approach Morgan immediately, having obviously been waiting for him. With cigar in hand, one of them ups the ante by telling Morgan simply to name his price. In so doing, he is indicating a willingness to pay dearly for Morgan's services—his driving skills, his discretion, and the use of his boat. Morgan's response is still no. The other associate then chimes in, offering to pay $1,000 for every person that is successfully smuggled (the currency is not specified—it could be dollars or pesos). Harry still says no.

The concept of price elasticity is crucial in understanding the negotiations between Morgan and the smugglers. The price elasticity of demand for Morgan's services is low. In other words, the smugglers are willing to entertain a broad range of prices because there is no one else in Havana with a boat as sturdy and reliable as Morgan's. It is a boat that can undoubtedly reach its destination and require no repairs while close to American shores. Also, Morgan has the reputation for being a fine captain, knowing the tides and the water depths better than any other fisherman.

Even though the smugglers tell Morgan to name his price, they do not really mean that they would pay any price whatsoever. If Morgan were to name a price for his service that is greater than the smuggler's revenue from the migrants (which is the money paid by individuals who are seeking to be smuggled) plus an acceptable profit for themselves, they would not agree to it. Therefore, while their price elasticity for Morgan's services is low, it is not perfectly inelastic.

At the same time, Morgan's price elasticity of supply is also low. He is unwilling to supply his boat services even when the price offered increases. Morgan is not motivated by monetary incentives. His sense of right and wrong, as well as his fear of going to jail, is the overriding sentiment at the time. Still, this does not mean that his supply is perfectly inelastic. Under the right circumstances, there is a price at which Morgan's services can be bought (those circumstances do not occur until later in the book).

Meanwhile, in his discussion with the smugglers, Morgan shows he is a rational fisherman. He points out to them that he makes his living with his boat. If he were to accept their offer, he could easily lose his boat, either due to an accident at sea or because it gets confiscated by the authorities. Either way, Morgan can lose his only means of livelihood. His boat is an integral part of his revenue calculation, as is the risk of getting caught. As a result, Morgan is undeterred when one of the smugglers tells him that, with all the money he can earn smuggling, he can buy a bigger and better boat.

Discussion Questions

1. Imagine you are a fisherman in a Cuban coastal town. Tourists pay you to take them fishing on your boat, and local residents pay you to transport them to the next town. How would you price discriminate in order to maximize your total revenue?
2. There are many islands in the Caribbean, all vying for North American tourists. Is Cuba a substitute for Jamaica or Barbados? Why or why not? Your answer should consider the U.S. trade embargo on Cuba that makes it illegal for Americans to travel to Cuba. Despite the embargo, some are nevertheless drawn to the island (for illicit business, curiosity, family reasons, and so on). How does the illegal nature of travel to Cuba affect the price elasticity of demand for such travel?
3. Smuggling illegal immigrants into the United States was lucrative for Morgan, and it continues to be a lucrative business, especially along the Mexico-U.S. border. In 2005, 1.2 million people were arrested for illegal entry while an unknown number got through, the majority with the help of middlemen or smugglers. Explain how those middlemen's revenues depend on the migrants' price elasticity of demand for transport to America.

Chapter 9

Consumption

Film: *CLUELESS*
Fiction: *GULLIVER'S TRAVELS*

KEY ECONOMIC CONCEPTS

Consumption is the term economists use to indicate spending by households. Consumers spend in order to get satisfaction.

Utility is the satisfaction derived from the consumption of a good or service. Rational consumers try to maximize the utility they get from everything they consume. However, as they do not have unlimited resources, they must consider their *income constraints*. Economists say that consumers maximize their utility subject to their income constraints.

Consumers distinguish between *total utility*, which is the accumulated satisfaction derived from increasing quantities of a good consumed, and *marginal utility*, which is the satisfaction derived from an additional unit of a good. Marginal utility refers to the change in total utility obtained from consuming one more unit of a good. Marginal utility tends to fall off as more of a good is consumed within a given time period, a concept embodied in the *law of diminishing marginal utility*.

Consumer decision-making entails comparing how much utility one gets per dollar spent and then consuming on the basis of that. This leads to the *utility maximizing rule*, according to which consumers will shuffle their consumption around until they achieve the same utility per dollar spent for each good they buy. In this way consumers make both short-run and long-run consumptive decisions that have different ramifications over time.

CLUELESS

Rated PG-13/1995/1 hr 38 min /Alicia Silverstone, Stacey Dash, Paul Rudd
Directed by Amy Heckerling

Cher (Alicia Silverstone) is a rich teenager in a Beverly Hills high school. She is a little ditzy and seems interested in little other than fashion. However, she has a good heart—she gives a new student a makeover and helps two teachers fall in love. This film is about her adventures with her best friend Dionne (Stacey Dash) and her relationship with her stepbrother Josh (Paul Rudd). At first, Cher and Josh clash whenever he visits, but over time they get to like each other as he begins to find her less superficial and she begins to think him less boring.

Economic Concepts in *Clueless*

Scene 1 (00:00–1:23)/ Minutes 0:00–1.23

Cher faces her biggest daily challenge in the mornings when she has to decide what to wear to school. She enters her huge walk-in closet, the size of most bedrooms across America. She then consults a mix-and-match computer program that allows her to compose her wardrobe. She begins by choosing the basics—for example, a skirt and blouse, and then the computer offers choices for matching shoes, sweaters, bags, and other accessories. Cher takes this choice of complements and substitutes seriously. Once satisfied with a particular combination, Cher walks to the other end of the room to retrieve the clothing from a mechanized rack, such as those used in dry cleaning establishments. At the push of a button, Cher's neatly hanging clothes glide past her to the humming sound of the moving rack.

During this daily morning ritual, Cher maximizes her utility subject to her time constraints. She gets satisfaction both from choosing her clothing with care as well as looking fashionable at school. She might be tempted to spend even more time choosing her clothes if she did not have to rush to school, but she is operating under a time constraint as her first class starts 90 minutes after her alarm goes off.

How did Cher's closet become so full of clothes? The answer lies in her passion for fashion. Cher derives utility from finding attractive clothing, purchasing it, and then wearing it. Cher maximizes her utility subject to the income constraint imposed by her father.

Together with her girlfriends, Cher spends a lot of time shopping. As a scene in *Clueless* shows, these young women walk around malls and streets, their hands filled with shopping bags. The expression on Cher's face conveys a sense of satisfaction with her consumption. When she finally goes home, it is because she has reached the point of diminishing marginal utility. Since she spends so much time shopping, the utility-maximizing rule allows us to infer that shopping gives her more utility per time spent than most other activities.

Discussion Questions

1. When Cher carries shopping bags, it conveys a sense of consumption and satisfaction. Yet, when a homeless woman (also known as a bag lady) carries shopping bags, it conveys neither consumption nor satisfaction. Use key economic concepts to explain this difference.
2. Cher's father is a successful attorney who works long hours and has large earnings. He does not use a computer program to select his daily attire. Use the concept of utility maximization subject to constraints to compare and contrast his morning dressing ritual with Cher's.
3. Cher has a monthly allowance that is used to pay for gas, entertainment, and clothing. Use the utility maximizing rule to explain her consumption pattern.

GULLIVER'S TRAVELS

By Jonathan Swift
New York: Barnes and Noble, 2003

Lemuel Gulliver is a doctor on a ship that travels to four imaginary destinations. Each destination is very different from the others. For example, in Lilliput he is a giant among tiny people while in Brobdingnag, he is the tiny one in a land of giants. In Laputa, carefree people are oblivious to their country's problems. The last country Gulliver visits is inhabited by Yahoos, who look similar to humans but are ruled by horses, the Houyhnhnms. In each of these destinations, Gulliver has memorable adventures.

Economic Themes in *Gulliver's Travels*

pp. 29–30

After a misfortune at sea, Gulliver is washed up, unconscious, on the shores of Lilliput, the land of the little people. When he regains consciousness, he realizes he has been captured and tied down by hundreds of tiny men who are now walking all over his body. They have arms and legs and eyelashes and fingernails—in fact, they are just like Gulliver except that they are minuscule. Soon a slightly bigger man approaches. By his body language, as well as the others' deferential reaction to him, Gulliver infers he is some kind of leader. Given that Gulliver is famished, not having eaten since before his shipwreck, he gesticulates by putting his finger in his mouth, hoping this bigger little man understands his needs and has the power to do something about them. It turns out that the man is in fact a leader, the Hurgo, the great lord of the Lilliputs, and yes, he understands Gulliver's desires.

The Hurgo immediately commands that ladders be put along Gulliver's sides so that hundreds of the tiny people can mount and walk towards his mouth to feed him. They carry food baskets overflowing with meat and bread. The animal carcasses are so tiny that Gulliver eats entire shoulders and legs, several pieces in each mouthful. Then he eats several loaves of bread at once, chewing quickly in order to satisfy his hunger, his gaping mouth asking for more and his stomach seemingly a bottomless pit.

Given that Gulliver is not paying for the food he eats, he does not have to consider price, and his utility maximization is not subject to an income constraint. Decisions pertaining to how much veal and beef to consume are based purely on utility.

At first, the marginal utility derived from each additional bite rises, as does Gulliver's total utility. After the initial pangs of hunger have subsided and Gulliver begins to feel satiated, his marginal utility begins to fall off. However, his total utility continues to increase as his mouth stays open to receive yet one more loaf of bread and yet one more whole chicken. Gulliver slows down when he reaches the point of diminishing marginal returns. Finally, when he begins to feel nauseous and his marginal utility becomes negative, he closes his mouth and turns his head away indicating to his hosts that he has finished eating.

Discussion Questions

1. Gulliver ate until he was satiated, without considering the price of the food. Yet, when people go to a restaurant, prices affect what they order. When reading the menu, how do consumers balance price with utility?

2. Joe loves the salad at Wendy's. It gives him more utility than salad from any other restaurant. His sister Jill derives more utility from a hamburger at Burger King than from anywhere else. Yet fast food restaurants such as Wendy's, Burger King, and McDonald's all offer a fast and relatively inexpensive way of satisfying hunger. Does this mean they are substitutes?

3. The Lilliputians fed Gulliver only meat and bread. According to contemporary nutritional guidelines, such a diet is unhealthy. Experts call on

Americans to increase their fruit and vegetable consumption at the expense of red meat. Such recommendations are troubling for Mr. Smith, whose eating habits include daily steak or fried chicken and no fruits or vegetables. How should Mr. Smith alter his thinking about utility so that his eating habits conform to health guidelines? (Hint: distinguish between short term and long term utility.)

Chapter 10

Production

Film: *GLADIATOR*
Fiction: *RUMPELSTILTSKIN*

KEY ECONOMIC CONCEPTS

All societies decide what is produced, how it is produced, and for whom it is produced. Production takes place with *inputs*, or *factors of production*, that are combined in a specific way to generate the outputs of goods and services that society wants. The outputs obtained from the given inputs can be seen in a *production function* that describes the maximum quantity of a good that can be created using different combinations and quantities of inputs. The total quantity of these inputs determines just how much production can take place.

The *production possibility frontier* is used to show graphically all the combinations of two products that can possibly be produced using all available inputs. If production occurs on the frontier, that implies maximum output is achieved; if it occurs within the frontier, then all inputs are not fully utilized. This production possibility frontier refers to the output of firms as well as countries.

Productivity is the measure of output per unit of input. Labor productivity, for example, measures how much one unit of labor can produce in one unit of time.

The *marginal product* refers to the change in total output derived from one additional unit of input. The *law of diminishing returns* states that marginal product of a *variable input* declines as more of it is employed together with a given quantity of *fixed inputs*. This law refers to the short run, namely the period of time when the quantity of inputs used in production cannot be changed (in the long run, all quantities can be changed).

In deciding which inputs to use in production, producers consider both the absolute price of inputs as well as their prices relative to each other. They also consider the productivity of the inputs.

GLADIATOR

Rated R/2000/2hrs 35 min/Russell Crowe, Richard Harris, Joaquin Phoenix
Directed by Ridley Scott
Winner of five Academy Awards, including Best Picture and Best Actor

When Roman Emperor Marcus Aurelius chooses Maximus (Russell Crowe) to succeed him, Marcus's enraged son Commodus (Joaquin Phoenix) murders his father. Commodus also arranges to have Maximus killed, despite his status as the most popular general in the empire. Commodus becomes emperor, and his rule is harsh. He believes Maximus is dead but he is wrong: Maximus is alive in North Africa. He is a slave who, after being purchased by a gladiator trainer, is brought to Rome to fight in the Coliseum. After much hardship, Maximus finally gets his revenge against Commodus.

Economic Concepts in *Gladiator*

Scene 9 (2:39–4:02)/ Minutes 48:39–50:02

The gladiator business was lucrative all across the Roman Empire. Spectators paid entry fees at amphitheaters to watch the gory events, speculators made bets on who would survive the longest, and sellers at concession stands sold drinks and food to the public. As with entertainment and sports in the twenty-first century, most people who were connected with the gladiator business thrived.

Proximo is one such individual. He runs a gladiator business across the Roman provinces of North Africa. Proximo is in the entertainment business; he is a producer of a service, namely gladiator fights. His goal is to profit from the slaves' death and dying, an event that people pay money to watch.

The factors of production that Proximo uses are animals, slaves, and land on which the games take place. Given the large size of his enterprise, Proximo has a consistent demand for both new slaves as well as for wild animals. He trains the slaves to be gladiators, knowing that the weak ones will die during the first match with the animals, while the strong ones might have multiple games in them. In any show, Proximo can use one of several production functions, including putting several weak slaves in the ring with one animal, or if the slave is particularly strong, he might pit a single animal against a single slave.

One day, Proximo approaches a slave merchant to discuss the purchase of slaves and animals. Their negotiations reveal information about how those inputs are valued by the buyer and the seller, both in absolute and relative terms. Proximo offers 2,000 (in an unspecified currency) for six slaves and 4,000 for two beasts. This implies that the price of one beast is higher than the price of one slave (333 and 2000, respectively). That price difference reflects, among other things, the longer life expectancy of the beast relative to the slave. Incidentally, one of the slaves Proximo wants to buy is Maximus.

The productivity of slave gladiators is measured by how much entertainment value they create per unit of time in the ring. The more they put up a fight, the greater the entertainment value for the audience. As a result, Proximo is willing to pay more for slaves who seem likely to fight harder. In fact, his interest in purchasing Maximus is tied to his assumption about Maximus's productivity. When Proximo notices the mark of the legion on Maximus's arm, indicating that he is a Roman warrior, Proximo knows that he is not buying a weakling.

The fixed input in Proximo's gladiator business is the amphitheater; the variable inputs are the beasts and the slaves. If Proximo keeps adding beasts and slaves without expanding into additional locations, the entertainment value that he produces will soon begin to fall off. Such diminishing marginal returns will occur because the ring will become so overcrowded with beasts and slaves that the gore will be obscured, producing insufficient entertainment value.

Discussion Questions

1. Across the Roman Empire, spectators watched gladiators fight with the odds stacked against them. Today, *Survivor* provides television viewers with human struggles under adverse conditions. However, the winner of *Survivor* gets $1 million while the winning gladiator gets to stay alive until the next performance. Compare and contrast these two forms of entertainment using key concepts.

2. In ancient times, spectators had to be in the same location as gladiators in order to watch the fight. Today, technology allows people across the globe to watch the Olympics on television while only a few watch them live. Explain this difference between ancient and contemporary entertainment industries using key concepts.

3. Proximo is in the death business, as is the Gibson Funeral Home. While both profit from death, there are some fundamental differences in

the production of their products. What are their inputs and outputs? How does each producer measure productivity?

RUMPELSTILTSKIN

By Jacob and Wilhelm Grimm
The Complete Grimm's Fairy Tales
New York: Pantheon Books, 1972

A poor miller lives with his daughter. He is a show-off and liar. He tells the King that his daughter knows how to spin straw into gold. Intrigued, the King orders the girl to be brought to the palace where she is given a room full of straw. If she does not spin it into gold by the next morning, she will be killed. Behind the closed door, the young woman cries until a funny little man called Rumpelstiltskin appears in the room and offers a trade: he will spin the straw in exchange for her necklace. They agree and the next morning the King is duly impressed. The next day the King repeats the offer, and again Rumpelstiltskin shows up, this time asking for the girl's ring. On the third day, the King tells the girl he will marry her if she can perform the feat once again. But on that night, Rumpelstiltskin demands her firstborn in exchange for his help. The miller's daughter, trying only to survive, accepts his offer.

Economic Themes in *Rumpelstiltskin*

pp. 264–65

The miller's daughter sits behind a locked door in the King's Palace, sobbing into her dainty hands. The room is bare except for a wooden chair, a spinning wheel, and numerous empty reels. These are the only resources she has at her disposal in order to produce all the gold the king wants. Conspicuously missing is a production function—the description of how to combine these inputs in order to produce the desired output.

Given that the young girl has no idea how to spin straw into gold, when the funny creature with the elongated green hat shows up, he seems to be the answer to her problem. Indeed, Rumpelstiltskin knows the production function, and he provides an additional input that neither the girl nor the king have—magic. In exchange for the girl's necklace, he works all night, and in the morning all the straw is spun and all the reels are full of gold.

When the curious king enters the room the next morning, he sees that the miller's daughter has produced a room full of gold, seemingly with the inputs that he left her. The King is thrilled with the girl's productivity.

In a mere eight hours, she had spun more reels than the most experienced weavers in the kingdom. And the output is gold!

But the King is too greedy to let the girl go home. The next night he leads her to yet another room with yet another spinning wheel, as well as more straw and more reels. The King wants the miller's daughter to increase her output of gold, to produce even more than the night before. He knows that if he gives her just more reels, or just more hay, she would quickly reach the point of diminishing returns, and the gold output could not grow to his satisfaction. He therefore increases all the inputs at her disposal, indicating a keen understanding of economics.

While she is given most of the inputs into the production function, that is straw, spinning wheel, and reels, the one that is missing—magic, has to be paid for. The first night she pays for that input with a necklace but during the subsequent two exchanges, the price of Rumpelstiltskin's service keeps escalating until finally, on the last night, the price is the young woman's firstborn baby. Her price elasticity of demand for Rumpelstiltskin's service is so low, given that her alternative is death, that she agrees to his price.

Discussion Questions

1. How is lying about one's skills during a job interview similar to the miller boasting about his daughter's capabilities? Explain using key concepts.
2. The phrase "making gold out of straw" has come to refer to accomplishing something seemingly impossible. Yet, over time societies accomplish feats previously thought impossible as new inputs and new production functions become available. Sending man to the moon is one such accomplishment. Can you think of others? Which factors of production were used that were not available one hundred years earlier?
3. One has to wonder how much the woman's necklace is worth if Rumpelstiltskin was willing to work all night and to produce heaps of gold in order to get it. How would you assign a value to the necklace based on Rumpelstiltskin's role in the production of gold?

Chapter 11

Costs

Film: *THE AVIATOR*
Fiction: *THE DA VINCI CODE*

KEY ECONOMIC CONCEPTS

Economists distinguish between several measures of cost. *Total cost* refers to the market value of all the inputs used to produce a good or service. These total costs consist of *fixed costs,* which are those that do not change when the rate of output changes (such as the cost of a sewing machine that is the same if one dress is produced or if ten are produced). Total costs also include *variable costs,* that is, those costs that change when the rate of output changes. An example of a variable cost is labor since more workers have to be hired to produce more output. The same is true for materials. Finally, *marginal cost* refers to the addition to total cost incurred by producing one more unit of output.

When a firm cannot cover its variable costs, it makes sense for it to cease production. The shutdown point of a firm occurs when the price of its product is equal to its average variable cost.

In addition to the cost of inputs, production costs also include the *taxes* that a business must pay.

In production, some costs are *explicit* while others are *implicit*. The former refer to actual payments made for the use of an input. Implicit costs are not actual dollar expenditures but infer the lost revenue that might have been attained if an alternative investment had been chosen. Economists call the implicit cost of any production the opportunity cost.

Economies of scale is a term used to describe the decrease in average costs that occur when more output is produced. This does not always happen. When it does, there is an argument in favor of large-scale production with big plants and abundant equipment.

THE AVIATOR

Rated PG-13/2004/2 hrs 50min/Leonardo DiCaprio, Cate Blanchett
Directed by Martin Scorsese
Winner of five Academy Awards

This movie is a fictionalized portrayal of Howard Hughes (Leonardo DiCaprio), an enigmatic entrepreneur who became one of the richest men of the twentieth century. His passion for films and airplanes led him to invest his own money and take huge risks in order to build a fortune. He had very innovative ideas, and his expansive empire focused the attention of the U.S. government in defining the boundary between competition and monopoly. He loved many women, including Katharine Hepburn (Cate Blanchett) and befriended many politicians. Over time, he became a recluse as he succumbed to a mental illness.

Economic Concepts in *The Aviator*

Scene 4 (00:10–2:45)/ Minutes 17:43–20:18

Howard Hughes is making a film called *Hell's Angels* based on World War I. It contains numerous air battle scenes, thereby combining his passion for film, aviation, and history in a single project. No wonder Hughes is happy, scuttling about the film set, directing, commenting, ordering, and utterly enjoying the experience. He continues to be happy, even when the filmmaking world changes in a nonreversible way: sound is added to film (the first commercial talking picture, *The Jazz Singer,* was released in 1927). Audiences love it and within a mere few months, films without sound become pathetically out of fashion.

Hughes is no quitter so he decides to add sound to *Hell's Angels*. That will add $1.7 million in expenses to an already over-the-budget project that has run into twenty-five miles of film. This additional expenditure will cover additional variable costs of production, including the labor time of technical staff and actors. Fixed costs, such as studio rent, will remain constant.

With furrowed brow and unbreakable confidence, Hughes instructs his reluctant financial adviser to go ahead and make the necessary financial arrangements. When the exasperated adviser tells Hughes they simply have no more money, Hughes replies, "We'll make it." He can afford to be so cavalier because he has other businesses from which continued profits can be used to cross-subsidize the film project. In addition, Hughes can cut costs by not paying himself an explicit salary and by excluding his implicit salary (his opportunity cost) from his cost calculation.

When the two men meet again in the studio at a later date, Hughes is told by the same cautious and increasingly uncomfortable financial adviser that the company is now losing $25,000 per day. Hughes is quiet for a few moments and then raises his head to ask, "What are my options?" The adviser tells him that the film production should be shut down because, by implication, not only are variable costs not being met but fixed costs are also not covered. The adviser hopes that after shutting down, Hughes can start to dig himself out from under.

"Mortgage every asset I have!" Hughes says calmly, his eyes fixed on a collision scene of airplane fighters in reel number 10. That's the kind of man Howard Hughes was.

Discussion Questions

1. Howard Hughes was one of the richest men in U.S. history who often invested his own funds into his entrepreneurial projects. How might that alter the way he, and others like him, value costs of production? Answer using terms such as implicit, explicit, accounting, and opportunity costs.

2. For Howard Hughes, flying was a hobby. He loved planes, flew them, and knew all about them. How might such knowledge of airplanes have come in handy when he purchased Trans World Airlines (TWA)? Which costs might have been reduced as a result of that knowledge?

3. Instead of adding sound to *Hell's Angels*, Hughes could have finished the film without sound or shut down production. Discuss the economic implications associated with each outcome.

THE DA VINCI CODE

By Dan Brown
New York: Doubleday, 2003

Robert Langdon is a Harvard professor of symbology. He happens to be in Paris when his colleague Jacques Sauniere is murdered inside the Louvre Museum. Langdon becomes involved in the investigation, together with the police chief and a famous French cryptologist, Sophie Neveu. Soon they discover that Sauniere was involved in the Priory of Sion, a secret society.

Since Leonardo da Vinci was also a member of this society, they begin to search his works for clues. Yet their efforts to unveil some historical secrets are met with resistance and obstacles as it becomes clear that important people want to stop them from uncovering the truth.

Economic Concepts in *The Da Vinci Code*

p. 26

Police Captain Fache takes Robert Langdon through the Louvre Museum to the gallery where curator Jacques Sauniere lies murdered on the floor. It is the middle of the night, and most museum lights are turned off. Elongated shadows cast by the artwork form a pattern that the two men crisscross while making their way to the scene of the crime. They pass from room to room, their steps echoing in the empty spaces. Langdon happens to look up. He notices security cameras mounted on the walls. Each room has them, as though screaming at the visitors, "Do not touch, big brother is watching!"

Langdon points to the cameras and asks the police captain if any of them are real. The policeman replies, "No, of course not." Why would a museum have security cameras that do not work?

The answer lies in the application of simple economics concepts. The museum administrators understand the difference between fixed costs and variable costs. Installation of the cameras is a fixed cost. It is the same whether the cameras function or not. However, the use of security cameras is a variable cost, incurred only when cameras are used. That cost is very high, as running the cameras involves filming through video in numerous locations and then surveying all the films. The Louvre's many acres of galleries would require several hundred technicians to monitor the feeds at all times. The labor costs involved in this process are prohibitive. Given the large number of rooms to be monitored, economics of scale exist but do not reduce the variable costs enough to warrant the use of cameras. Therefore, total costs of security are decreased when fake cameras are used.

That does not mean there is no security at the Louvre. To the contrary, there are two types of security that are always in effect. The first is associated with the fake cameras whose mere presence acts as a deterrent since most people assume they function. The second system of security is less expensive and has come to be used widely across museums all over the world. It is called containment security and entails the automatic sealing of exits from any gallery where a piece of artwork is moved. In this way, thieves are kept in rather than kept out. While this system has high fixed costs, including set-up costs, its variable costs are significantly lower than those associated with functioning security cameras.

Discussion Questions

1. Mr. Joe Average wants to install a security system in his suburban home. The home protection industry provides many options including cameras, motion detectors, and alarms. Irrespective of which option is chosen, each installation includes a sign by the front door stating that the home is protected. Having read *The Da Vinci Code*, Mr. Average decides to decrease his costs by buying only the sign. Explain his reasoning, and explain why the security companies are unlikely to sell only signs.

2. Museums in wealthy cities tend to have more valuable art collections than museums in poor cities (for example, the Metropolitan Museum in New York has more expensive paintings than the hypothetical Community Museum of Little Town, Oklahoma). Explain this phenomenon in terms of the costs of buying and showing art (supply) as well as costs of viewing the art (demand).

3. The Louvre Museum houses what is possibly the most recognized painting in the world, the *Mona Lisa* by Leonardo da Vinci. In order for more people to appreciate the painting, museums arrange exchanges and the *Mona Lisa* travels on loan to museums across the globe. However, she must be insured against theft, damage, and other unforeseen events. Is such insurance a variable or fixed cost? Who do you think bears that cost, the Louvre or the hosting museum?

Chapter 12

Profits

Film: *TARZAN THE APE MAN*
Fiction: *BABBITT*

KEY ECONOMIC CONCEPTS

Producers strive to maximize *profits*. Since profits are the difference between the total cost of producing an item and the total revenue earned from its sale, producers try to increase the gap between the cost and the revenue.

Economists distinguish between *accounting profits* and *economic profits*. The former take into account only explicit costs whereas the latter also consider implicit costs (such as opportunity costs). For economists, economic profit is a more realistic assessment of true profits than accounting profit.

TARZAN THE APE MAN

Rated NR/ 1932/99 min/Johnny Weissmuller, Maureen O'Sullivan
Directed by W. S. Van Dyke

This is a classic film that gave rise to numerous other Tarzan and Jane films and stories. In it, Jane Porter (Maureen O'Sullivan) is a young woman who travels to Africa to join her father, an explorer. She gets there just in time for an expedition into the jungle in search of ivory. They set off and soon after Jane gets abducted by Tarzan (Johnny Weissmuller), a human who has lived all his life in the jungle. Jane falls in love with him and, given his knowledge and love of wild animals, he ends up helping her and the members of the expedition survive in the jungle.

Economic Concepts in *Tarzan The Ape Man*

Scene 4 (00:00–1:07)/ Minutes 11:41–12:47

Jane travels all the way from England to southern Africa for a surprise visit to her widowed father, James Porter, whom she has not seen in a long time. He is an explorer and has been holed up in a remote African village with his associate Holt. When Jane, frazzled and sweaty after her long voyage, walks through the door of their shack, Porter is thrilled. Despite his joy at seeing Jane, he tells her she must immediately return to the safety of her English countryside life.

Explaining the reason he wants her to leave, Porter drops his voice so no one can hear. It is a secret that the very next day he and Holt will depart on a dangerous expedition. It will take them through the hostile jungle in search of the elephant graveyard. "The elephant graveyard?" Jane asks dubiously. It turns out that Mr. Porter has identified the location of the famous graveyard where, according to legend, elephants go when they are old and want to die in peace. It is the largest concentration of elephant skeletons in the world and, therefore, the largest concentration of elephant tusks. The ivory from elephant tusks is a luxury item in demand across the globe. It is used to make ornaments and horns and in some places is believed to have medicinal powers.

If Mr. Porter manages to find the elephant graveyard, he will have access to a huge number of elephant tusks. As he explains to Jane, he will become the world's largest supplier of ivory. In his calculations, Porter is making assumptions about the magnitude of the supply of ivory, as well as about the extent and consistency of global demand.

Jane's father has estimated that he will get 1 million British pounds if he finds the elephant graveyard (such earnings are significant even in the twenty-first century, and they were even more so in the 1930s when this story takes place). It is not clear if Mr. Porter is referring to revenue or profit. If he is referring to revenue, then Porter will have to subtract his costs from the one million in order to estimate his expected profits. These costs include ship and land transport, expedition equipment, removal, and marketing of tusks, among others. However, if Porter is referring to profits, then he must have already taken those costs into account, and it follows that his total revenue is in excess of one million.

In either case, it is clear that Jane's father is driven on this expedition by the possibility of making profits. One assumes that Mr. Porter is savvy enough to be calculating his economic profits, namely the profits derived after he has calculated the opportunity cost of his time. In other words, if he could be earning twenty pounds per day at his job back home, and the expedition lasts thirty workdays, he must add 600 pounds to his total costs even if he is not explicitly paying himself. If he fails to make this calculation, then his implicit costs have not been covered and he is dealing with accounting profits.

Discussion Questions

1. Jane's father is seeking riches based on the myth of an elephant graveyard. Can you think of other examples of people investing in searches (based on dubious information) with the goal of reaping profits (hint: check this book's table of contents)? In these cases, how is the length of the search related to the expected profits? Answer using implicit and explicit costs.
2. In the early twenty-first century, numerous Chinese firms relocated to African countries where they now produce their output. What can you infer about the costs of production in Africa? What does this heightened Chinese activity across Africa imply about expected profits?
3. Since *Tarzan* was filmed in the 1930s, a lot has changed in the ivory industry. In an effort to preserve elephants, in 1990 it became illegal to trade in ivory. However, poachers who kill elephants to take their tusks still exist, and ivory continues to be smuggled out of many countries including Zimbabwe, Kenya, and Congo. What must be true about profits in the ivory trade if poachers continue this risky trade?

BABBITT

By Sinclair Lewis
New York: Barnes and Noble, 2005

George Babbitt is a real estate businessman in Zenith, a Midwestern town. He is successful, has a devoted wife, three children, and a lovely house. Yet he is dissatisfied. It seems as though all he does is make money so that he can buy things. To escape the consumerism that has taken over his life, Babbitt has an affair and even tries to make it in politics. He wants to find happiness but doesn't know how.

Economic Concepts in *Babbitt*

pp. 44–46

The following deal described in *Babbitt* illustrates how George Babbitt speculates in the real estate market in order to make profits.

Linton is a neighborhood that is undergoing transformation as new ownership leads to renovations that are transforming decrepit blocks into pleasant residential homes and thriving businesses. For a realtor, a changing neighborhood implies profits that are not only possible, but also likely.

Babbitt learns about a grocer, Purdy, who wants to open a butcher shop immediately adjacent to his grocery store. Babbitt investigates the surrounding properties and learns that Purdy did not yet buy the adjoining property that is up for sale. Babbitt sees an opportunity for profit and gets to work right away. He advises his friend and mortgage broker, Conrad Lyte, to immediately buy the lot for $11,000. Soon thereafter, Lyte puts the property back on the market and he, together with Babbitt, tells Purdy that there is a lot of demand for the property. It would be such a shame, they tell Purdy, if someone else got the property and opened a combination grocery-and-meat market right next door. They all know such an outcome would put Purdy out of business.

Having thus laid the groundwork, Lyte then offers to sell Purdy the property for $24,000. Purdy is shocked. He complains that a similar property in the neighborhood just sold for $8,500. However, despite his complaints, Purdy understands he has little choice. In other words, his price elasticity of demand is low. Babbitt intercedes to make a counterproposal: he will convince Lyte to lower the price to $23,000, of which $5,000 must be put down immediately with the rest to be mortgaged. Babbitt adds that he will convince Lyte to provide a very good mortgage rate.

In the end, Purdy gets the property next door where he builds a butcher shop. He passes some of his costs on to the consumers of Linton who have to pay slightly higher prices for their beef and chicken. Readers are told that Lyte makes over $9,000 in profit. His selling price was $23,000 and his purchase price was $11,000, leaving him with a difference of $12,000. We can infer that the total costs of the real estate transaction, such as drawing up the paperwork, doing a title search, and transferring title to the property, amounted to $3,000. Among his additional costs is Babbitt's commission, which was $450—a sum worth a lot more in 1922 than today, as well as the opportunity cost of his time when he engaged in extensive conversations with both Babbitt and Purdy.

Discussion Questions

1. How does the size of Lyte's profit depend on Purdy's price elasticity of demand?

2. A real estate boom has changed Miami's skyline. In addition to office buildings, numerous high-rise condominiums now dot the landscape. These condos are typically purchased by empty nesters, professional singles, snowbirds, and speculators. In addition, the demand for condos in

Miami is also fueled by South Americans who want to own property in the United States. It follows that Miami's construction companies are keenly interested in the economic well-being of Argentines, Chileans, and Venezuelans. Explain.

3. Lyte is a real estate speculator who buys and sells real estate and makes a profit on the transaction. He is different from a professional realtor, or real estate agent, who facilitates the deal between buyer and seller for a fixed percentage of the deal. How does that compare to the profits that a speculator such as Lyte expects?

Chapter 13

Efficiency, Productivity, and Innovation

Film: *WALL STREET*
Fiction: *THE ADVENTURES OF HUCKLEBERRY FINN*

KEY ECONOMIC CONCEPTS

Efficiency in production refers to obtaining the maximum output of a good from the resources used. When producers are inefficient in their production process, it means that they are using the same amount of inputs but are getting less output.

Productivity of resources measures how much output is produced per unit of time. Productivity and efficiency tend to increase when *innovation* occurs in the production process. Innovation refers to the use of more modern production techniques that use newer *technology* or that combine inputs in new ways.

Since innovation in production usually entails the adoption of more machinery and capital inputs, it then implies that fewer workers are hired. Such labor-saving production results in *structural unemployment*, meaning that workers lose their jobs because their skills are no longer relevant in the labor market.

WALL STREET

Rated R/1987/2hrs 5min/Michael Douglas, Charlie Sheen
Directed by Oliver Stone
Winner of Academy Award for Best Actor

Gordon Gekko (Michael Douglas) is a wealthy and unscrupulous businessman who buys and sells companies. He takes a liking to the young Bud Fox (Charlie Sheen), a risk-taking stockbroker, and begins to tutor him in the ways of the business world. Bud falls under Gekko's spell, loving the attention as well as the money he is making. In his efforts to please Gekko, Bud reveals that the airline where his dad works, Blue Star, is facing bankruptcy. As Gekko moves ahead with a buyout of the airline, Bud begins to question his goals and methods. These involve insider trading, an illegal activity, and force Bud to reevaluate what is important in life.

Economic Concepts in *Wall Street*

Scene 13 (6:05–6:45)/ Minutes 1hr 25:13–1hr 25:56

Bud has arranged a meeting with representatives from Blue Star's three unions to give Gekko a chance to present his plan for the failing airline. The meeting takes place in Bud's luxurious Manhattan apartment where the art is bold and the walls are painted in dark hues. Bud and Gekko are both wearing deep navy suits, white shirts, and serious ties, their Gucci shoes and gold watches advertising their wealth. Bud's dad, a mechanic at Blue Star, together with a flight attendant and a carpenter, look oddly out of place seated on the sleek Italian furniture.

After telling a mildly funny anecdote intended to break the ice, Gekko cuts to the chase. He tells the Blue Star union representatives that their employer has losses of $20 to $30 million, that dividends have been cut to zero, and the company is squeezed by the major airlines. Its managers are about to declare bankruptcy and are certain to use bankruptcy laws to break up the union and fire the workers. But Gekko has an idea that will save the airline and make everyone a lot of money. He plans to buy the airline and modernize it.

At this point Gekko turns the floor over to Bud. The young man paces with excitement as he explains the economic rationale behind modernization while the flight attendant munches on a carrot stick. The first step, he says, is that computer software be updated in order to enable more efficient inventory management. Such technological innovation will result in higher productivity of reservation workers while improved efficiency in the reservation system will result in higher sales. Inventory management, he says, will also enable more dollars to be squeezed out of every seat so that, using price discrimination, an individual who is willing to pay $375 for a ticket does not get it for $75. Computerization will thus increase the load factor on each flight by some 5 to 20 percent, which will in turn raise revenue by some $50 to $200 million.

Bud's father is at first skeptical and later becomes downright despondent, clearly stating his disagreement with the proposal. His concern is that profit-maximizing innovation will hurt the union workers because it will introduce labor-saving production methods. Men and women he has worked with all his life will find themselves structurally unemployed, displaced by technological change. He anticipates that workers will be forced to take wage cuts that, although touted as temporary, will in fact turn out to be permanent. He distrusts individuals such as Gekko who are motivated by greed and have no interest in the men and women of the union.

Deeply disappointed with his son, Bud's father walks out of the meeting and into Manhattan's dark night.

Discussion Questions

1. Last time you booked an airline ticket, it is likely you used the Internet. Yet not too long ago, reservations were made by airline ticketing agents who called a central number to check availability and wrote tickets out by hand. How has innovation in booking methods increased labor productivity of both ticket agents and business travelers?
2. The Internet has decreased the demand for all travel agents, not just airline ticketing agents. What kind of unemployment did they experience? Despite innovation across the travel industry, some travel agents have survived. Why is there still demand for their services? In other words, why doesn't everyone satisfy his or her travel needs with the Internet?
3. Bud's glamorous girlfriend prepared snacks for the guests. She made popcorn in a microwave and mixed the cookie batter with an electric mixer. How are the microwave and mixer labor-savings inputs used in meal preparation? What is their effect on the girlfriend's labor productivity and efficiency in the kitchen?

THE ADVENTURES OF HUCKLEBERRY FINN

By Mark Twain
New York: Penguin, 1986

This story is set in the 1830s and is narrated by a thirteen-year old boy, Huck Finn. Huck teams up with Jim, an African-American slave as they both try to escape—Huck from his drunkard father and Jim from slavery. Together they float on a raft along the Mississippi River. When Jim is captured, Huck must decide whether to save him. He is a poor, uneducated boy who does not know the ways of the world, and the experience makes him think about the inhumanity of slavery. He had become friends with Jim and had begun to view him as a human being with feelings and compassion, rather than a piece of property to be bought and sold in the slave market.

Economic Concepts in *The Adventures of Huckleberry Finn*

pp. 130–31

Huck is a poor white kid with torn-up jeans and a head full of disheveled hair. Jim is taller and older, his jeans also full of holes that reveal patches of rough black skin. Big and small, black and white, old and young—this unlikely couple of such noticeable contrasts makes its way downriver, floating on a hastily constructed raft.

The Mississippi River is murky in color, and oversized oak trees cast their shadows at its edges, adding to its darkness. Huck and Jim are quiet, not calling attention to themselves in the hopes that they will elude capture and, after many days and nights, float to a new life, away from Huck's abusive father and the reign of slavery. They lie motionless during the scorching daylight, communicating mostly with their eyes, and when night falls, they cook some food under cover of darkness while whispering softly to each other. They eat fish when they are lucky enough to catch some. Their stomachs grumble and their mouths salivate as they patiently hold their fishing lines for hours on end, in anticipation of a morsel or two to satisfy their hunger.

Huck and Jim both have low labor productivity. This is evident not only in their inefficient way of obtaining food but also in their incompetent mode of transport. Indeed, in their capacity as fishermen, Huck and Jim's catch per hour would be significantly higher if they adopted more sophisticated fishing gear (in other words, if they used more capital inputs to complement their labor). Similarly, in their capacity as travelers, Huck and Jim could reach their destination faster if they used a more advanced form of transportation than a raft. For example, as passengers on a steamship, they could reach their goal within twenty-four hours rather than the week or so they expect to spend rafting.

However, Huck and Jim cannot be more productive fishermen or travelers because they lack the means with which to purchase improved fishing equipment and steamboat tickets. In addition, their labor productivity is also hampered by the secret nature of their activities. After all, they are fugitives; all economic activity in which they engage, be it fishing or traveling, must of necessity be invisible.

While lying still on the floating raft, Huck and Jim scan the landscape and undoubtedly marvel at the evidence of technological change a few dozen yards away. Sharing the river with them is the most novel form of water transportation, the steamboat that chugs by at speeds neither Huck nor Jim have seen before. Both are mesmerized by the sight of these huge bodies moving noisily across the water, coughing up steam and producing fireworks when their sparks fly out from the chimneys. Steamboats represent innovation over the traditional way of moving goods and people across water, namely with sail power. A steamboat uses steam propulsion and as such, represents the use of capital in production. It can therefore achieve greater output (that is, the transport of more people and goods per unit of time) than other forms of river transportation. The productivity of both the machine as well as the workers who operate it is higher than on a raft.

The introduction of an engine that does the work previously performed by rowers is labor-saving technological change. It results in structural unemployment as those who previously rowed boats are no longer in demand.

At one point on their southern journey, Huck and Jim find themselves surrounded by a fog so thick that they can hardly see each other at their opposite ends of the raft. They cannot even gauge how close the passing steamships are. This leads them to perform a cost-benefit analysis in order to decide their future action. Should they make noise, calling attention to themselves, and thereby signaling to the passing ships to avoid them? Such behavior would protect them from a collision that would certainly result in immediate death. While the benefit of calling attention to themselves is obviously high, the cost would also be high: Huck and Jim might be caught and returned to the very circumstances they worked so hard to escape.

After careful consideration, they choose to avoid collision, as its negative consequences were immediate and more probable. Huck and Jim assemble all the tin pans they have on the raft and frantically beat on them with any and every utensil they can find. This is a labor-intensive way of producing protection. It has come to be replaced with horns that transportation vehicles have and that drivers use to signal their existence, often for protection against larger vehicles.

Discussion Questions

1. In terms of safety, traveling by rafts alongside steamboats is similar to driving a Vespa scooter on a highway filled with SUVs. Are the two also comparable with respect to efficiency and productivity in transport and travel?

2. There has been a lot of technological change in the shipping industry. What have the steamboats described by Huck Finn been replaced with? Discuss these replacements with respect to efficiency and productivity.

3. Innovation often takes place in response to safety concerns. For example, the sparks emitted by a steamship were a fire hazard and thus were eliminated in the later model ships. Can you think of other products that were improved upon because of the safety concerns they raised?

Chapter 14

Property Rights and the Rule of Law

Film: *JERRY MAGUIRE*
Fiction: *THE CATCHER IN THE RYE*

KEY ECONOMIC CONCEPTS

In order for a market economy to function successfully, individuals and firms must be able to own property. The right to own *private property* is a fundamental tenant of the capitalist economic system, one that distinguishes it from command or traditional systems.

Without a legal environment that protects private property, ownership is meaningless. *Property rights* refer to laws about property. Such laws define property ownership and the rights of people and firms to have property and do what they like with it, including sell it, rent it, or pass it on as inheritance.

Contracts are drawn up to clearly define property rights. Societies have institutions, such as courts, to enforce those contracts. In societies based on the *rule of law*, contracts protect businesses and individuals. In the absence of such protection, rational people will be uneasy about taking risks, such as starting a new business or investing in an existing one.

Intellectual property rights refer to intellectual property, namely nontangible material, such as music and film and other creative endeavors. *Patents* and *copyrights* protect owners and creators of material by giving them exclusive rights that prevent others from inappropriately using their ideas.

JERRY MAGUIRE

Rated R/1996/2hrs 19min/Tom Cruise, Renée Zellweger, Cuba Gooding Jr.
Directed by Cameron Crowe
Winner of one Academy Award

Jerry Maguire (Tom Cruise) is a sports agent whose cutthroat methods make him very successful. However, when he develops a conscience and tries to induce his entire firm to give up their ugly competitive practices, he gets fired. His girlfriend leaves him, and his colleagues become distant. Only office worker Dorothy Boyd (Renée Zellweger) believes in him and becomes his assistant when he sets up a solo practice. Most importantly, all of his clients abandon him with the sole exception of football player Rod Tidwell (Cuba Gooding Jr.). In the end, Maguire, together with Boyd and Tidwell, shows that it pays to be the nice guy.

Economic Concepts in *Jerry Maguire*

Scene 11 (0:00–3:45)/ Minutes 44:43–48:28

Jerry Maguire travels to the NFL Draft to negotiate deals between teams, players, and endorsers. It is a high-stress atmosphere in which the stakes are high.

Jerry seeks out his client Cushman (also known as Cush) to discuss a proposal. He enters Cush's hotel room to find the young football player relaxing on the sofa, playing a guitar and humming a made-up song. Cush is currently the most popular player in American football, and he knows it. All the teams want him on their side, and all the advertisers want to pay big bucks for his endorsement. Cush's father Matt, who is also his adviser and agent, is beaming at his son's success. And Jerry is happy too, as he has some important news to convey to his client.

Jerry has negotiated a great deal for Cush with San Diego: a seven-year contract for $30 million plus an $8 million signing bonus. Jerry came through for his client and is proud of himself. However, he does not get the reaction he expected from Cush. No shouts of joy, no champagne, no patting on the back. Jerry becomes suspicious, and moments later he remembers: he only has a verbal agreement with Cush and his dad, nothing on paper. Jerry reaches for a yellow legal pad to quickly write up a contract, one that formally gives him the right of representation—one that has a signature.

But it is too late. Matt and Cush both stall, and after a few hems and haws, they reveal the devastating news. Just one hour ago, they signed a contract with Bob Sugar, Jerry's main rival, granting him the right to represent Cush. Jerry learns the hard way that a verbal agreement cannot stand up to a written agreement in a court of law. Even though Matt had said to him in an earlier scene, "My word is stronger than oak," the contract he signed with Sugar is even stronger than that.

When football players and team owners sign contracts, property rights come into play. The team owner buys the rights to the player's abilities, skills, and talent. The holder of those rights can then sell the team player or lend him out to other teams.

Discussion Questions

1. Before their wedding, John and Tracy promise to love each other forever and to share everything. Ten years later, in the divorce proceedings, John refuses to share his family inheritance with Tracy, denying there was a verbal agreement. To avoid such problems, some modern couples are signing prenuptial agreements to be enforced in case of divorce. Using key concepts, explain what such agreements do.
2. Despite an unspoken agreement between students and professors, some students plagiarize when they write research papers. In order to help identify cheating, some professors use a service called Turnit-In that checks student papers for lifted sentences. Use key concepts to explain both plagiarism as well as the monitoring service.
3. People who wouldn't steal a CD from a music store find nothing wrong with downloading songs from the Internet. How do you explain that behavior? Which laws are being broken?

THE CATCHER IN THE RYE

By J. D. Salinger
Boston: Little Brown and Co., 1991

Holden Caulfield is sixteen and suffering from teenage angst that is compounded by the death of his younger brother. Although parents and teachers look the other way because of his trauma, Holden pushes too far and ultimately gets expelled from boarding school. As he heads home to New York City, he begins a three-day adventure that is recounted in this coming-of-age book. He meets with some friends and professors and meanders the streets of Manhattan before finally going home to his parents. The scope of Holden's existential feelings show teenage anxiety was similar in the 1950s to what it is today.

Economic Themes in *The Catcher in the Rye*

pp. 69–70

In the smoke-filled jazz club, dim lights hang low over crowded tables, while a brighter bulb lights up the podium for the musician, when there is one. Holden swaggers in, trying his best to look older and more self-assured than he is. He takes a seat at a table for four and surveys the room. Not too far away is a table with several young women of indeterminate age, their hands clutching half-filled glasses rimmed with lipstick stains. Holden tries to catch the eye of one of them, the blonde with dimples. He desperately wants to make an impression, to show her how cool he really is.

Just then the waiter comes by to take his drink order. Dropping his voice an octave, Holden orders a scotch and soda, adding, "Don't mix it!" in the way he has often heard his mother say. The waiter is not impressed. Despite his efforts at seeming blasé, Holden is asked to produce proof of his age. Instead of backing down, Holden stares at the waiter with the bow tie and gives him a dirty look as though to indicate, "How dare you insult me, of course I'm over the drinking age limit." Sensing the waiter's intransigence, Holden changes his order to a Coke. He does not even bother glancing at the blonde girl who had overheard the conversation with the waiter. There is no way he can impress her now.

The waiter explains to Holden that there are rules he will not break. He is referring to United States law that stipulates liquor cannot be sold to individuals under the age of twenty-one. Authorities enforce the underage drinking law that Holden is trying to break by conducting periodic checks in establishments that serve liquor. If the waiter is caught selling scotch and soda to young Holden, he would lose his job and the jazz bar would be fined. The owner of the bar, although holding property rights on a private establishment, must abide by laws that regulate activities on his premises. By opening a jazz bar and acquiring a liquor license, he is in effect entering into a contract that stipulates he will not serve alcohol to minors.

Discussion Questions

1. Some underage students carry fake ID cards that state they are over twenty-one and therefore old enough to purchase alcoholic drinks. Similarly, some waiters and bouncers don't inspect the IDs carefully enough to detect the deception. Using key concepts, explain what the students and bouncers are doing.

2. New research has shown that an ingredient contained in red wine, reservatol, has health benefits. This might explain why the French, who

regularly consume red wine, have fewer cases of heart disease than Americans. Do you think information like this affects alcohol consumption laws? What determines drinking age laws in a country?

3. In some two dozen states across the country, Mr. Boozer cannot buy a martini with his brunch because of the so-called Blue Laws. These laws are remnants of bygone days when governments prohibited the sale and consumption of alcohol on Sunday mornings on moral grounds (at the time, it was thought that all people should be in church on Sunday mornings). Use the concept of property rights to explain why the existence of Blue Laws causes conflict between the owners of liquor licenses (such as liquor stores and restaurants) and special interest groups concerned with morals.

Chapter 15

Externalities

Films: *THE PELICAN BRIEF*
Fiction: *JURASSIC PARK*

KEY ECONOMIC CONCEPTS

The processes of production and consumption affect more people than those who are directly involved in producing and consuming. Benefits often flow to others, as do costs. The benefits and costs that are borne by individuals who have nothing to do with production or consumption are called *externalities.*

Negative externalities are the by-products of consumption or production that have negative effects on some people. An example of negative externalities is air pollution whose cost is borne by those not involved in production. *Positive externalities* are the by-products of production or consumption that have positive effects on others, such as the benefit reaped when one's neighbor invests in beautiful landscaping.

The existence of externalities leads economists to distinguish between public and private goods. *Public goods* are those that can be consumed by many people and whose consumption does not exclude consumption by others. No one can be excluded from consuming a public good (such as the light from a lighthouse). *Private goods* are goods consumed only by those who buy them while all others are excluded. A coat and a restaurant meal are examples of private goods. *Free riders* are people who benefit from a good without paying for it. Since it is impossible to charge individuals when they consume public goods, no private producer will supply them and their provision is left to the government.

The existence of externalities leads economists to distinguish between private costs and benefits and social costs and benefits.

THE PELICAN BRIEF

Rated PG-13/1993/2 hrs 21min/Julia Roberts, Denzel Washington
Directed by Alan J. Pakula

While doing research on environmental issues, law student Darby Shaw (Julia Roberts) comes across an interesting connection between the murders of two very different Supreme Court judges. She writes up her findings in a brief (called the Pelican Brief) that she shares with her professor who, in turn, passes it on to a friend in Washington. Soon afterwards, the professor becomes the first of many who get assassinated as some very important people try to suppress Shaw's findings. In desperation, Shaw contacts a reporter, Gray Grantham (Denzel Washington), to help her. Following clues, they uncover a conspiracy that links environmental protection and oil interests and implicates numerous members of government.

Economic Concepts in *The Pelican Brief*

Scene 23 (2:44–5:55)/ Minutes 1hr 13:47–1hr 16:58

Shaw and Grantham are hiding in a hotel room, out of sight from the multiple assassins trying to obstruct their search for evidence. This is the first opportunity Shaw has to walk Grantham through every detail of the conspiracy that led to the murder of two Supreme Court judges. The Manhattan lights spill into the room where Shaw sits, barefoot legs curled up under her, speaking slowly and softly. Her eyes are bloated from crying, her hair is pulled back, and her face has not seen makeup in weeks. The gray sweatshirt and pants that hang on her thin body seem to indicate comfort but no, Shaw is not comfortable; on the contrary, her fear for her life has become all-encompassing. Grantham's tape recorder is recording her words while his hand scribbles additional notes on the Marriott stationery. Shaw's discussion of the Pelican Brief continues deep into the night until they are both drained and exhausted.

At the root of Shaw's story is a powerful and wealthy man called Victor Mattiece who has made and lost several fortunes in the oil business. In 1979 his company hit a bonanza—it discovered huge quantities of oil in Terrebonne Parish, Louisiana. The problem was that in order to bring drilling equipment to the site and then take the oil out, Mattiece's workers needed to pass through a protected natural reserve.

That reserve is the home to osprey, geese, and especially the brown pelicans. All these birds are severely endangered due to thirty years of air and soil pollution (especially contamination by DDT, a highly potent chemical used in nearby manufacturing and farming). In order to save the pelicans from extinction, the federal government declared the reserve a protected site, thereby preventing any activity that would alter the balance between nature and the pelicans. In so doing, the government created a public good—a territory that people can enjoy and consume its beauty, without paying for its upkeep.

Since the land is societally owned, it is not up for sale or lease to private individuals, such as Mattiece, who seek to use it for private purposes in the pursuit of private interests. In pursuing those interests, his drilling equipment would indeed alter the very balance between nature and animals that the government is trying to preserve. Drilling for oil is an economic activity that results in negative externalities, as the use of heavy machinery and the installation of oil pipes entails large-scale land clearance, which inevitably disrupts the life of the pelicans. In other words, the production process would create a negative by-product on land adjoining the oil site, including the land that is federally protected.

Mattiece needs to procure special government permission to use the reserve or else he cannot drill for oil. Someone very powerful in Washington would have to make a special dispensation to allow Mattiece to circumvent the rules applied to federally protected land. In order to achieve his goal, Mattiece becomes the president's biggest campaign contributor. Soon after the president is elected, Mattiece receives the right to gorge through the reserve.

But soon thereafter, an environmental group called Green Fund files a lawsuit to stop his activities. Mattiece spares no expense as he battles in court against these underfunded environmentalists. Just before Darby Shaw writes her now famous Pelican Brief, the lawsuit has reached the Fifth Circuit Court of Louisiana and will in all likelihood proceed to the next step, namely the Supreme Court of the United States. Mattiece is aware that there are two justices who are particularly environment-friendly: Rosenberg and Jensen. Although differing on many other issues, they have consistently voted the same way when it comes to issues of pollution, environment, and nature preservation. Eliminating them would enable Mattiece's friend, the president, to name two new judges to the bench—judges who would be less concerned with endangered pelicans. To Mattiece, funding a double murder seems like a small price to pay for the possibility of earning billions of dollars in an oil venture.

The question now is whether Darby Shaw and Gray Grantham will survive long enough to leave the Marriott Hotel and collect enough evidence against Mattiece to go public with the above story.

Discussion Questions

1. Comment: In a time of rising oil prices, should we not be more concerned with increasing the supply of oil than with allowing brown pelicans to fly freely over Louisiana's marshes? Increasing the supply of oil could help reduce the price of oil and therefore do more for the American population than saving a bunch of birds.
2. Over 60 percent of Alaska's territory is owned by the federal government. When oil was first discovered, Native Alaskan land claims were raised. Are the interests of the Native Alaskan population better served by the production of oil or the maintenance of a pristine environment? Does your answer depend on whether the Alaskan population is required to share its oil revenues with the other forty-nine American states? (There is no right or wrong answer.)
3. The state of Louisiana is home to Terrebonne Parrish where brown pelicans are concentrated. Louisiana is also the state devastated by Hurricane Katrina that in 2005 caused damage in excess of $100 billion. By 2007 many residents of the New Orleans area still haven't rebuilt their homes and businesses. Why not divert federal resources from environmental protection in Louisiana to post-hurricane reconstruction? Answer in terms of social and public benefits and social and public costs.

JURASSIC PARK

By Michael Crichton
New York: Ballantine Books, 1991

Michael Crichton's electrifying thriller shows how greed and technological innovation can have deadly environmental repercussions. Specifically, scientists discover a method for cloning dinosaur DNA that entrepreneurial businessmen then use to hatch real animals. The plan is to disperse these animals throughout an amusement park in Costa Rica that is expected to draw many visitors and generate huge profits. However, while still in the early stages, the dinosaurs become violent and as a result, many people die together with the entrepreneurial dream.

Economic Concepts In *Jurassic Park*

pp. 64–68

Off the coast of Costa Rica lies a seemingly deserted island of hills and valleys covered with dense tropical foliage. On the surface, the landscape seems eerily untouched by civilization, but right under the surface, state-of-the-art innovations are being put into place to house the world's most unique amusement park/zoo. This state of the art facility is the brainchild of a company called InGen that has secretly funded research of animal scientists interested in the past, such as paleobiologists and DNA phylogeneticists. The culmination of their work is the cloning of dinosaurs after grinding up large quantities of bones for the extraction of DNA. When *Jurassic Park* begins, the construction of a resort facility on the island is almost completed and a modern transportation system is poised to carry visitors around to the best dinosaur viewing sites.

InGen has purchased the island with the goal of building the single biggest tourist attraction in the history of the world. It has done so in order to make a profit. InGen can pursue profits on its private property in any way it wants. Given that it has legally obtained the deed to the property, InGen can build on it, parcel it out, pave it and resell it. Despite the fact that some may find the idea of an amusement park inhabited by cloned animals unappealing or even offensive, InGen does not seem to have broken any law.

The island is a private good. To the extent that visitors want to visit, they can do so only as payers. Its remoteness and lack of unsupervised access by airplane or boat means that entry is easily controlled and free riders are prevented from coming.

While it is easy to understand that the amusement park is a private good, it is less obvious that the dinosaur eggs are private. After all, they have been created from scattered bone fragments that belonged to no one in particular. Yet, the scene described in the selected pages indicates no ambiguity on this question. InGen's cloning of dinosaurs has been patented and therefore protected from imitation. Nevertheless, an emergency meeting of the board of directors of its competitor, Biosyn, has been called in order to discuss how to circumvent that patent. Their chief scientist suggests that some of InGen's intellectual property should be stolen and then altered sufficiently to get around the patent laws. How will Biosyn engage in such industrial espionage? A disgruntled employee and improperly disposed trash were mentioned as possibilities.

In exercising its property rights, InGen has changed the island's physical environment. It has built an artificial shallow lake two miles long in the center of the island, thereby clearing large tracts of jungle. It has also installed miles of fencing to keep animals in and visitors out. The transportation systems and routes also necessitated vast land clearings. Finally, InGen introduced animals that are new to the setting and whose daily roaming and feeding habits are sure to change the flora and fauna of the island. The positive externalities associated with the new amusement park include, for example, increased employment for nearby villagers as well as increased economic activity in the airplane and boat businesses. The negative externalities of the amusement park include environmental degradation and pollution associated with high volumes of visitors.

Discussion Questions

1. The readers are not told if Costa Rica has environmental laws that prevent activities with negative externalities. If it does, how would those laws have altered InGen's construction plans for the amusement park?
2. Pollution is partially to blame for global warming (the increased temperature of the earth's atmosphere). One likely consequence of such warming is the melting of glaciers and arctic icecaps. The subsequent rise in sea levels would pose a future danger to oceanfront communities. Comment: If businesses that pollute compensate residents of oceanfront communities, global warming is not a problem.
3. The Grand Canyon National Park is managed by the U.S. Department of the Interior. Given its popularity, the Grand Canyon is often congested. Might congestion be eliminated if the park were managed by a private company, such as in *Jurassic Park*? If the park becomes a private good, does that of necessity imply that benefits are only private? Isn't a decrease in congestion a social benefit?

Chapter 16

Firms

Film: *THE PERFECT STORM*
Fiction: *THE FIRM*

KEY ECONOMIC CONCEPTS

There are three types of firms in the United States. A *proprietorship* is a firm owned by a single individual while a *partnership* refers to joint ownership by two or more people. In both types of firms, the owners also operate the firms, receive all the profits, and are responsible for the firms' liabilities.

That is not the case when a firm is a *corporation*, namely a legal entity whose ownership is divided into shares. A corporation's legal status as a business with *limited liability* for its owners means that the owner's liability is limited to his or her investment in the firm. By limiting liability, the owners are protected so they cannot lose their personal assets in case of lawsuits or bankruptcy.

In corporations there is a *separation of ownership and control*. In other words, in large corporations it is typically managers, rather than shareholders, who control and manage day-to-day operations of the firm.

All firms seek to *maximize profits*. They strive to increase total revenue and decrease total costs. When they do not succeed in covering their variable costs, they shut down. That is different from *insolvency*, which happens when a firm's liabilities exceed its assets. Insolvency can lead to *bankruptcy*, namely a declaration by a court of law that a firm cannot meet its debt obligations.

THE PERFECT STORM

Rated PG13/2000/2hrs 9 min/ George Clooney, Mark Wahlberg, Diane Lane
Directed by Wolfgang Petersen

This film is based on real events that happened in Gloucester, a small town in New England where most economic activity centers around fishing. The Gloucester Coast Fisheries Company is the major employer. Billy Tyne (George Clooney) is one of the many captains who work for the company. Recently his catch has been unsatisfactory. In desperation, Tyne decides to risk one more fishing trip even though it is late in the season. He takes his boat out further than most fishermen go, and he is rewarded with a phenomenal catch. The problem is that the ice machine breaks down and without it, the fish will spoil. Tyne realizes he needs to turn around and go home immediately in order not to lose the catch. However, if he does, he will take his boat and crew into the biggest storm of the century.

Economic Concepts in *The Perfect Storm*

Scene 2 (3:30–4:56)/ Minutes 6:14–7:42
Scene 3 (1:42–2:32)/ Minutes 9:39–10:39

It is an autumn day in 1991, and the Gloucester harbor is overwhelmed by activity. Boats are docking after extended fishing expeditions. Fishermen unload their catch, captains weigh their fish, and family members joyfully greet their long-absent loved ones. This frenetic activity takes place under the shining midday sun and amidst the stench of fish guts that permeates the entire town. Everyone, no matter what their role on the pier, is grateful that all the ships returned safely.

But Captain Billy Tyne is gripped by an additional emotion: disappointment. Used to extraordinary success on the seas, he now watches his competitors bring in larger catches than his and walk away with larger checks than his. That doesn't feel good, nor does the verbal beating he gets from the owner of Gloucester Coast Fisheries Company for his poor performance.

The Gloucester Coast Fisheries Company is a proprietorship with a sole owner who is referred to simply as Boss. It is likely that he incorporated to limit his personal liability. His assets are far too large and his business far too risky not to have legal protection in case of a lawsuit.

The company's assets include a large warehouse, numerous fishing boats, and minor capital equipment, such as scales, refrigerators, and forklifts. Captains and their crews are hired to take the company boats out to sea. Those boats are fully equipped to help the fishing crew catch fish, clean them on board, and keep them iced. Once off board, the company provides weighing and packaging services, as well as transportation to out-of-town markets.

There is no separation between ownership and control in the Gloucester Coast Fisheries Company. When Tyne and Boss discuss issues of hiring and day-to-day operations, the latter makes on-the-spot executive decisions pertaining to hiring and wages, without needing to consult anyone. For example, Boss threatens to fire Tyne because he is not bringing in sufficient fish. He says, "I like you, but I like my boat better. If you can't make her pay, I'll find someone else who can."

To avoid getting fired, Tyne proposes to take one last trip before closing down for the season. He wants one more opportunity to improve his mediocre fishing record. Tyne is undeterred by the approaching bad weather, with its stormy skies and oversized waves. Tyne is so motivated to reverse his losing streak that he even plans on taking the boat farther out to sea than he ever did before, past the Grand Banks, into waters that have not been overfished.

When Boss hears about the Grand Banks, he shakes his head. His opposition stems from his concern that the boat will be damaged and perhaps even lost. The loss of a fully equipped boat represents a significant expense for the company. Add to that the possible economic costs of losing a crew, including probable lawsuits, and Boss must consider carefully the financial and solvency issues before letting Tyne take his boat. "It's too risky," he says.

On the day depicted in the scene, the economics behind the daily fishing operations are clearly revealed. Tyne's crew brings in 21,000 pounds of fish that sell for $3.50 per pound for a total of $73,500. The operating costs (including tackle, bait, and fuel) amount to $35,000 and are deducted from the revenue. The remaining $38,500 is then divided as follows: one half goes to the company that owns the boat and equipment while the other half is divided among the crew. The captain gets a double share, four crewmen get a single share each, and the one rookie on his first voyage gets three-quarters of a share. Tyne receives a record low check of $5,923.76 and duly signs the ledger, his baseball cap shading his week-old stubble.

Discussion Questions

1. There have been several tainted fish scares and alarms about mercury fish poisoning, all of which resulted in a temporary decrease in demand for fish. What kind of fishing firms are best able to handle changes in demand and why?

2. As the owner of Gloucester Coast Fisheries Company, Boss bears the risk for company assets. For this reason he is reluctant to let Tyne take his

boat into the dangerous waters beyond the Grand Banks. What creative arrangement might Tyne propose to address Boss's concerns and induce him to change his mind?

3. In commercial deep-sea fishing, boats are typically equipped with refrigerated storage facilities so that fish are cleaned aboard and unloaded ready for sale. If the refrigerator breaks down while the ship is at sea and the fish are spoilt, who is responsible for the loss: the ship owner, the captain, or the crew? Answer for all three types of firms.

THE FIRM

By John Grisham
New York: Dell, 2003

When Mitch McDeere, a recent graduate of Harvard Law School, begins looking for a job, the offers are immediate. He signs on with a Memphis law firm (Bendini, Lambert and Locke) that offers him a hefty salary with great benefits. After he and his wife Abby move to Memphis, Mitch begins to notice suspicious behavior at the firm. Soon thereafter, the FBI approach him with a request for help. Investigators believe his firm is linked to the mob, and they want Mitch to spy for them. They have leverage: Mitch's brother Ray is serving time in jail, and the FBI will consider early parole if Mitch cooperates. As he begins spying for the firm, the members of the firm suspects him. In the meantime, bodies start piling up and Mitch struggles to save his life and his marriage.

Economic Concepts in *The Firm*

pp. 9, 11

Mitch is being interviewed for an associate position at Bendini, Lambert and Locke in a hotel room with yellow-flowered wallpaper and Queen Anne furniture. Although he regrets the burger swallowed quickly on a nervous stomach, Mitch is surprisingly calm. He is, after all, at the top of his graduating class. And anyway, the partners sitting before him are not intimidating, and their firm seems different from the cutthroat New York firms he interviewed with.

Oliver Lambert, one of the senior partners, goes to great lengths to explain just how different the firm is. It is midsized, employing some forty lawyers and about as many in staff. While Lambert doesn't spell it out, it is likely that the firm is a limited liability partnership. From what Mitch can gather, the partners own the law firm, and decisions seem to be made by the managing partner whom he has yet to meet. This is different from the other law firms that interviewed Mitch. They were much larger, with many more attorneys and staff, and were set up as limited liability corporations that hired CEOs and CFOs to make decisions. The small size of Bendini, Lambert and Locke appeals to Mitch.

As one of the firm's selling points, Lambert explains that its earnings per lawyer are higher than any firm of its size or larger. Although this might indicate that each lawyer is extremely productive (which they are, Lambert states proudly) and/or that each works longer hours than usual (which they do, he claims), there is another matter that distinguishes his firm from others. In order to maximize its profits, the firm chooses its clients very carefully. It only takes on rich clients—be they corporations, banks, or wealthy individuals. In other words, its clients are exclusively those who are able to pay the firm's hefty prices and who are used to paying their bills on time. The law firm does not take on clients who seem like they cannot pay, and it immediately drops those who do not pay on time. And since the firm specializes in international taxation, a highly profitable specialty, the pool of clients that satisfies these criteria is large and stretches across the globe.

Then, breaking into a broad smile, Oliver Lambert reveals to Mitch that there is another, even more important reason for his firm's success. The partners have a policy of striving to make each lawyer happy. They believe that if they provide the atmosphere of a close-knit fraternity, where the top takes care of the new hires and generously meets their needs, the young lawyers will be grateful, loyal, motivated, and therefore highly productive. It seems that the firm's managers strive to create a work environment that is so comfortable, exciting, and compelling for the lawyers that they never want to leave. Rather than fostering complacency, such an environment has been found to decrease turnover, saving the firm the expense of repeated training costs. All that compounds the firm's profitability.

After this description of the firm, Lambert leans back in his chair with a twinkle in his eyes. He senses that young Mitch is impressed.

Discussion Questions

1. Comment: Whether a firm sells fish (such as the Gloucester Coast Fisheries Co.) or legal services (such as Bendini, Lambert and Locke), it maximizes profits according to the same economic rules.

2. Although Lambert doesn't mention bankruptcy, he and Mitch both know how common it is among U.S. firms. What does he say that implies bankruptcy is an unlikely future outcome for Bendini, Lambert and Locke?

3. Lambert claims that his firm is like a fraternity because the partners look out for the young hires. In what way are fraternities like firms?

Chapter 17

Perfect Competition and Monopolistic Competition

Film: *YOU'VE GOT MAIL*
Fiction: *SHOPAHOLIC TAKES MANHATTAN*

KEY ECONOMIC CONCEPTS

Firms that produce eggs behave differently from firms that produce cars, and economists refer to the *market structure* to explain that difference. Industries can be classified into four market structures on the basis of their firms' characteristics. At one end of the spectrum is *perfect competition* in which there are many firms that compete with each other in supplying an identical (or homogeneous) good. Each firm is small relative to the total market. No firm dominates as each is too small and insignificant to have an impact on prices, no matter how much it sells on the market. As such, it has no *market power*.

All firms in perfectly competitive markets are *price takers* and set their price according to the market price. Independent price setting does not make sense: if one firm raises its price, there is no demand for its product as its numerous competitors will provide the identical good for less. At the same time, if a firm lowers its price, it will not cover its costs. Either way the firm will not survive and will be forced to exit the industry.

As there are no *barriers to entry* in perfect competition, firms easily enter and exit the industry, resulting in a changing composition of firms within an industry. As firms begin making profits, others will enter the industry and the increased supply of output will drive prices down; as firms begin incurring losses, many will exit the industry and the decrease in supply will drive prices up. As firms enter and exit the industry in response to changes in their profits, the long-run equilibrium is reached in which profits of all firms are zero.

Most competitive industries do not share the characteristics of perfect competition. Instead they are part of *monopolistic competition,* a market structure characterized by barriers to entry (they are low but nevertheless existent) and the production of similar (but not identical) products. Producers pursue *product differentiation* by accentuating (and advertising) the differences among their products (examples include Wendy's and Burger King). Because of product differentiation, monopolistically competitive firms have some market power (they face downward sloping demand curves). The more they can convince consumers that their product is different, the greater their sales and the more market power they have. Firms with market power can sustain profits in the long run.

YOU'VE GOT MAIL

Rated PG/1998/1hr 59min/Tom Hanks, Meg Ryan
Directed by Nora Ephron

In this love story with important economic lessons, Joe Fox (Tom Hanks) is the owner of a large book chain, and Kathleen Kelly (Meg Ryan) is the owner of a small independent bookstore. They begin to chat over the Internet and, as each is involved in an unfulfilling relationship, they easily develop a friendship and over time fall in love. However, they do not know each other's identities. Meanwhile, Joe is about to open one of his stores in exactly the section of Manhattan where Kathleen's shop is located. When her business begins to fail, she is distraught and spills out her heart to her new Internet friend. It is Joe who first figures out that Kathleen is the owner of the little bookshop but decides not to reveal his identity until their relationship is on solid footing.

Economic Concepts in *You've Got Mail*

Scene 7 (00:00–00:37)/ Minutes 18:00–18:37

Kathleen, an avid reader, is the sole proprietor of a small bookstore called The Shop Around the Corner. She hires two equally passionate book lovers to help her run the shop, and together they happily provide reading material to grateful and loyal customers. But all that changes one day, the day they learn that an uninvited neighbor is moving in just down the street—the Fox Superstore, a national chain of bookstores. Kathleen's workers fear the competition will drive them out of business.

It is a windy autumn day when they step outside their shop to assess this competition. There is nothing subtle about the construction site with its huge signs already enticing customers with promises of sales. Kathleen stands flanked by her workers, but her facial expression is unmistakably different from theirs. They wear concern on their faces while she seems serene and at peace. How can she not share their worries?

The answer lies in her understanding of product differentiation.

Kathleen explains to her staff that the new bookstore will not hurt them because they are not in the same business, and they are not selling the same product. When selling her books, Kathleen provides personal service and individual attention. She caters to neighborhood customers whose tastes she knows well and whose children roam comfortably in her stacks. She is the neighborhood's reading adviser, bringing her vast knowledge of books to bear on each choice buyers make. Moreover, Kathleen's service is provided in a cozy shop with traditional paneling and inviting chairs that mimics a comfortable living room. Surely all that cannot be duplicated by Fox in a huge, anonymous store in which high-turnover, minimum-wage salespeople (who probably don't even like to read) advise buyers on book choices.

What Kathleen describes to her coworkers, albeit in lay terms, is the concept of product differentiation. While there are many sellers of books, they do not all sell the same product. The book industry is monopolistically competitive, characterized by numerous firms all striving to modify the product they sell so that consumers will believe it is sufficiently different and hence buy it, over and over again. Kathleen chooses time-intensive personalized attention as the distinguishing characteristic of the service she sells. For her, a book is not just a book.

However, that characteristic is unlikely to protect her in the long run from the Fox Superstore. Given that it is part of a huge chain, Fox has the market power that The Shop Around the Corner lacks. Its sheer size enables it to offer discounts, to stock a large inventory of books, and to expand into the sale of related goods, such as calendars, notebooks, and pens. These attractions are likely to pique the curiosity of even the most loyal of Kathleen's customers. In the absence of some further creative product differentiation on her part, it is likely that her sales will decrease, her profits will erode, and her revenue will no longer cover rent and payroll. This scenario, so realistically portrayed in *You've Got Mail* has played out across American cities when booksellers, such as Borders and Barnes & Noble, have crowded out small bookshops.

Discussion Questions

1. At the beginning of the film, Kathleen believes she can survive the pressures of competition because of the service she provides to book buyers.

Discuss the service component in the differentiation of products sold by Honda dealerships, airlines, and hair salons.

2. Using key concepts, explain how Kathleen's little bookshop might have survived if she had been the only seller of books in Spanish?

3. Competition is characterized by easy entry and exit of firms in the industry. It is easier to imagine The Shop Around the Corner exiting the industry than Fox. Why? Even if Fox moved away from the neighborhood, why is it unlikely to exit the industry altogether?

SHOPAHOLIC TAKES MANHATTAN

By Sophie Kinsella
New York: Dell Publishing, 2002

Becky Bloomwood is a financial guru on British television. It is hard to believe that she advises people on how to spend and save their money when she is a compulsive shopper. She carries huge debt on her credit cards, and her checks usually bounce. She borrows in order to pay back debt. She shrugs it all off, rationalizing that she simply cannot resist a Prada bag (or anything else). While juggling to manage her personal finances, her boyfriend announces that he must move to New York for work. He invites her to come along. Having heard so much about the shopping possibilities in Manhattan, Becky readily accepts his offer. They move to New York, and Becky's reckless shopping continues unabated. However, it is harder to manage her credit cards so far away from home. She almost gets caught—almost but not quite.

Economic Concepts in *Shopaholic Takes Manhattan*

pp. 143–144

Becky and Luke have moved to New York. While Luke works long hours to establish his reputation on his new job, Becky looks for ways to fill her days. The problem is that she has few interests other than shopping. She is, after all, the quintessential consumer, buying things she needs as well as those she doesn't need. The entire act of buying thrills her—the excitement of identifying an object of desire, palpating it with her fingers, whipping out a credit card, and then triumphantly walking away with her possession firmly in her grasp. Becky is exactly the type of consumer that firms in the apparel industry love.

Soon after her arrival to Manhattan, Becky signs up for a bus tour of the city. She is not drawn by tourist attractions, such as Rockefeller Center, the Empire State Building, or the Statue of Liberty. Rather, she wants to get an overview of the shopping areas. While tourists from all over the world ooh and ahh when their guide, Christoph, points left and right out the two-story bus windows, Becky cannot concentrate. How, she wonders, can she be expected to concentrate on the historical development of Manhattan's street grid when just down the street a multitude of shops vie for her attention.

Right in front of them is Saks Fifth Avenue, one of the most famous department stores in the world. Becky blissfully tries to imagine floor after floor of dresses and shoes and bags. Her pulse races; her breathing quickens. So many opportunities for her to part with her money! Then she notices Gucci, and then, just to the left, the largest GAP she's ever seen. New York has an agglomeration of clothing shops hard to find anywhere else in the world. And all the while, fashionable consumers walk up and down the street with their designer bags and fancy sunglasses, providing Becky with still more clothes and accessories to covet.

The shops that draw Becky's attention are both small and large and sell both generic and designer clothing. They are part of the monopolistically competitive apparel industry in which product differentiation is paramount. Brand names convey information about product differences. For example, Armani Exchange goods are youthful with flair while Saks appeals to older, wealthier buyers. Both shops have successfully diversified their products and, with the exception of shopaholics like Becky who like everything, they appeal to distinct shoppers.

On that particular day, Becky's clothes-shopping fantasies are just that—fantasies. At the moment, there is only one item that she has in fact purchased, namely her tour ticket. The only industry she is actually participating in is the monopolistically competitive city tour industry. Dozens of tour operators offer day trips around Manhattan. Given the existence of people who share Becky's interests, as well as the low barriers to entry in the tour industry, operators have differentiated their product and offer specialty apparel shopping trips (it is likely that Becky did not sign up for such a trip because she had imperfect information).

Discussion Questions

1. Are button-down cotton shirts from Old Navy and J. Crew homogeneous products?

2. Years ago, people wore clothes made by a member of their household or by a local seamstress. Today, few people sew their own clothes, and individualized tailoring is prohibitively expensive. Using economic concepts, explain why most clothing is now factory produced.

3. If it is easy to enter the city tour business, why has no firm to date offered a tour of the city's supermarkets?

Chapter 18

Monopoly and Oligopoly

Film: *DO THE RIGHT THING*
Fiction: *ATLAS SHRUGGED*

KEY ECONOMIC CONCEPTS

If perfect competition is at one end of the spectrum of market structures, *monopoly* is at the other end. It is fundamentally different from perfect competition insofar as it contains only one firm. That one firm is the entire industry as there is no other producer of a similar product. Monopolies take *product differentiation* to the extreme as they provide goods for which there are no available substitutes.

Barriers to entry are so high in monopolistic industries that no other firms can enter. If they could, there would be no monopoly. The barriers are maintained due to a variety of factors. For example, the firm night have sole access to inputs of production. Alternatively, the government might have given it monopoly status through copyright and patent protection of its product or the method used to produce it. Also, *economies of scale* might be so large that production only makes sense when the firm is big (then the firm is a *natural monopoly*). As a result of such high barriers to entry, monopoly status is maintained and monopoly profits can be greater than zero in the long run.

By providing a unique product, a monopoly has the most *market power* that a firm can have. It is a *price setter*, making prices that others in similar industries then follow. Monopolies often set prices that some people consider exploitative, and sometimes antitrust policies are brought to bear on the producers in order to modify their pricing methods. *Antitrust policies* are government efforts to encourage competition by making collusion illegal.

In the real world, pure monopolies are less common within industries than within a geographical location. In other words, we are more likely to find monopoly in a small town with a single fast-food restaurant than in the national fast-food industry. In the real world, oligopolies are more common.

Oligopoly is a market structure characterized by a small number of competing firms. These firms are often large, making use of economies of scale. Barriers to entry are high but not impregnable. Firms provide similar products, although each strives to differentiate its product and gain a larger share of the market by stressing the differences of its product over others. Oligopoly pricing shows interdependence since no single firm can set prices oblivious to the pricing behavior of the others. *Price leadership* occurs if one firm is the biggest or the strongest, and it sets a price that others follow. But even the biggest firm must consider the pricing response of its competitors when setting its price.

When *collusion* occurs among oligopolies, firms agree not to compete against each other or to engage in destructive competition. Instead, they agree on charging the same price for their products. Collusion, and the *cartel* that is formed when firms collude, is against the law in the United States. If it weren't, the consumers of their products would face higher prices.

DO THE RIGHT THING

Rated R/1989/2hrs/Spike Lee, Danny Aiello, John Turturro
Directed by Spike Lee

Italian-American Sal (Danny Aiello) owns a pizzeria in a tough Brooklyn neighborhood where he makes Italian food with his two adult sons, Pino and Vito. To make deliveries, he hires a local kid, Mookie (Spike Lee). Racial tensions always fester just below the surface and on one particularly sweltering summer day, they boil over and a riot erupts. It all began when some of Sal's customers suggested he replace photos of Italian stars on his walls with African-American celebrities. After Sal takes offense, saying he can hang whatever he wants on his shop walls, Buggin' Out, a neighborhood kid and customer, calls for a boycott. It doesn't take much for the neighborhood shopkeepers, customers, and police to become deeply involved in a situation that soon spins out of control.

Economic Concepts in *Do the Right Thing*

Scene 9 (00:00–00:54)/ Minutes 57:36–58:30

Sal and Pino sit at a table for two that abuts the floor-to-ceiling windows facing out to the street. The pizzeria is empty, and they are taking a midafternoon break. The pizza dough is already laid out in clumps on the kitchen countertop to be molded into shape closer to dinnertime. The pepperoni and mushrooms are sliced, and the tomato sauce is simmering on low heat. Sal is tired, hunched over the Coke he is twirling absentmindedly with his hands. Pino is in his undershirt, his gold chain rubbing up against his flour-dusted apron. The heat is unbearable—it is hard to breathe, and their sweaty forearms stick to the vinyl tabletop.

"Dad, just sell this pizzeria, and let's get outta here," Pino urges his father. His plea is not new. Pino hates the neighborhood where he spends his days. Unlike his father, he never made friends and has always treated his black customers with disdain. The feeling is mutual as Pino wears his racism on his sleeve.

In response, Sal gives him a lesson in economics. He explains that their pizzeria has no competition in the neighborhood. Sal is the only producer of a product that is unique in the neighborhood, namely Italian food. Therefore, Sal is a local monopolist. Although a mere subway ride away there are numerous other pizza parlors, experience has shown that customers do not take that subway ride. There is no motivation as the price of a slice is not lower nor is the product superior. Sal can count on local demand because the local consumers of Italian food value the convenience Sal provides.

Although Sal is a monopolist, he does not exploit his market power by setting unreasonable prices. In deciding how much to charge for a slice of pizza, Sal undoubtedly considers other restaurant options his consumers have, such as a single hamburger and hot dog establishment. He also considers the nature of the local demand for pizza as well as its price elasticity. Even without studying economics, Sal knows intuitively that if he were to charge $10 per slice of Sicilian pizza, his customers would withdraw their demand, even if there were no other pizza parlors in the neighborhood.

Although he enjoyed monopoly status for over twenty-five years, Sal did not amass sufficient profit to enable him to retire and move to Florida. On the other hand, he is not destitute, having managed to provide adequately for his family. He still provides employment for his two adult sons.

While other industries exist in this sleepy and economically underactive section of Brooklyn, they tend to be oligopolies rather than monopolies. For example, in the hair-cutting business, there are several barber shops as well as a handful of beauty salons. These shops rely on locally available skills. No one in the neighborhood has a monopoly on hair-cutting techniques. As a result, barriers to entry based on skills supply are low.

By contrast, barriers to entry based on skills are high in the pizza business. Pizza production requires skills that are rare in the black neighborhood and abundant in the Italian neighborhood. That explains why Sal has no competition from his black neighbors. But why doesn't he have competition from Italians? In other words, why are there no competing pizzerias owned by Italians who, like Sal and his sons, cross neighborhood boundaries every day?

The answer again lies in barriers to entry. When Sal first opened his pizzeria some twenty-five years ago, relations between Brooklyn's Italian and black populations were peaceful. Since then, animosity and distrust between the two groups has grown. Italians have come to believe that the black part of town is dangerous. That perception of danger is a barrier to entry in the restaurant business, and it has prevented Italians from opening pizzerias alongside Sal's.

Instead, those Italians with skills in pizza production have set up shop in their own neighborhood. Not one of those shops is unique. For that reason, when Pino tells his dad, "Let's get outta here and set up shop in our neighborhood," Sal shakes his head. He explains that in the Italian neighborhood, the pizza industry is saturated, and he is better off staying where he is a monopolist.

Wearily, Sal ends the discussion with his son by stating that Sal's Famous Pizzeria is here to stay. He has no idea that a massive boycott of his shop will soon spread like wildflowers across the streets of Brooklyn.

Discussion Questions

1. It is estimated that seven million pizzas are consumed in America each day. How many pizzerias are there in your neighborhood? Why do you think there are not more?
2. If you had the possibility of opening a restaurant in your neighborhood, what factors would you consider? How might you distinguish your product in order to capture a greater share of the market?
3. Boycotts of stores and products are organized in order to induce a change in behavior. When some neighborhood kids organize the boycott of Sal's pizzeria, the resulting decrease in demand for pizzas could force Sal into bankruptcy, even if he is a monopolist. If the boycott succeeds in closing down the pizzeria, who else will be hurt besides Sal?

ATLAS SHRUGGED

By Ayn Rand
New York: Signet Books, 1992

This book is about a group of industrialists and how they deal with the extreme economic hardship that is taking place in the United States during an imaginary time. Two of these are Dagny and Jim Taggart, sister and brother who have inherited and must now run Taggart Transcontinental, the world's largest railroad network. Dagny is the stronger of the two and disagrees with her brother on all the fundamentals of running the company. Two men play a role in Danny's life: Hank Rearden, the owner of Rearden Steel, and Francisco d'Anconia, a South American playboy. The fortunes of these individuals are all affected by increased government involvement and regulation and ultimately nationalization of industries.

Economic Concepts in *Atlas Shrugged*

p. 50

A secretive meeting of four influential men is under way in the most expensive barroom in New York City. The ceiling is low, as though to trap all the important conversations that take place within its walls. There are not even any windows lest some information seep out—only slanted vents that allow a trickle of daylight to peep through. Although located on the roof of a skyscraper, the bar is entered by a winding narrow staircase that gives one the impression of entering a cellar. This bar is undoubtedly hard to get to, making the arrival of the choice few who can afford its services a treacherous feat that underscores their exclusivity. And exclusive they are, these four men seated at one of the tables, speaking in hushed voices as though the weight of the world is pressing on their chests.

Under discussion is the U.S. steel industry. One of the men at the table, Orren Boyle, explains to the others how and why the industry, previously an oligopoly, is turning into a monopoly. Boyle is angry because his company, Associated Steel, is one of the firms being pushed out of the industry. He tells the following story.

In the past, the steel industry consisted of several competing firms. Each purchased iron ore from a variety of sources. Each then transformed the ore into steel products that it marketed across the country. According to Boyle, his Associated Steel had the most modern plant, as well as the most efficient organization (in fact, it was awarded the Industrial

Efficiency Award just last year). It was the principle producer of steel. As a result, his company was the price leader in the industry.

Now, the output of the once supreme Associated Steel has dwindled. The reason is that the company can no longer purchase the principle input into production, namely iron ore. The lack of ore supply is a national problem, one that is due to exhaustion of many mines. No one can get iron ore. No one except for Rearden Steel, that is.

Rearden Steel is a competing steel company. Its owner, Hank Rearden, had the foresight to buy numerous iron mines over time. By buying mines, he assured himself a constant supply of ore. He also ensured that other steel companies would have to buy from him, at his prices. By controlling the supply of this crucial input, Rearden was always able to deliver his product on schedule. The more he delivered when others failed, the more demand there was for his product, and the more economies of scale enabled him to further expand his output.

Now, Rearden Steel is the only firm left standing while other producers are going out of business. In other words, an oligopolistic industry has become a monopoly.

Rearden Steel is undoubtedly a monopoly. It produces a unique product for which there are no substitutes. At the same time, it is a product that faces a huge demand. Indeed, steel is crucial for train rails and, in the era depicted in *Atlas Shrugged,* trains were the main form of transportation for goods and people.

As with all monopolies, the steel industry now has insurmountable barriers to entry. The first of these results from Rearden Steel's control of the supply of inputs. Other firms cannot produce steel goods unless they can purchase iron ore. The second type of barrier is due to economies of scale. The nature of steel production requires a huge initial investment. As other firms go out of business and their assets dwindle, no new firms have been able to afford the initial investment required to enter the industry.

Boyle is animated at this point, and the three men at the table listen carefully. He asks them whether it is fair that so many companies (including his) should be put out of business just because one man has property rights on important natural resources.

Jim Taggart is one of the other men seated at the table. He swishes the whiskey in his glass, ice cubes clinking loudly. He wonders what fairness has to do with economics, but he doesn't want to burst Boyle's bubble. Not yet. Where is this conversation going, he wonders.

He gets an answer to his question soon enough. Boyle wants Taggart to use his political influence to convince the government to introduce antitrust policies. Such policies would obliterate Rearden's advantage in the steel industry. Boyle doesn't want to cooperate with Rearden or to contemplate price interdependence of their products, or even to collude. He simply wants to take away Rearden's monopoly status.

Will Taggart agree? And will lawmakers listen to him? Boyle believes so, but only if he can convince them that monopolies are destructive to society. That is what he sets out to do.

Discussion Questions

1. Comment: Rearden should not be punished for having the foresight to buy ore mines. To the contrary, he should be rewarded. Our country needs more entrepreneurs like him, people who think ahead and act quickly.

2. Angelina Jolie will be playing the beautiful Dagny Taggart in a film version of *Atlas Shrugged.* Comment: It is appropriate that she should star in a film about monopoly since she herself has a monopoly on beauty.

3. America's antitrust laws were designed to prevent consumers and small producers from abuse by large domestic monopolies. But times have changed. We are now part of a global economy in which unregulated foreign monopolies compete with our restricted producers. Some have argued that perhaps it is time to reexamine our antitrust policies. If you were in charge of such reexamination, what factors would you consider, and why?

III

MACROECONOMIC TOPICS

Chapter 19

Economic Growth

Film: *SWING SHIFT*
Fiction: *MAJOR BARBARA*

KEY ECONOMIC CONCEPTS

Gross domestic product (GDP) refers to the sum of all final goods and services produced in a country during one year. Since economists cannot add up quantities of diverse goods, such as apples and tractors, they instead add the market values of apples and tractors, all given in dollars.

When an economy experiences an expansion in production of goods and services, that implies *economic growth* has occurred. Growth refers to the economy's ability to produce increasing quantities of new goods and services.

The maximum output that a society can produce given its resources is called the *potential GDP.* Usually some resources are unemployed at any given time so society achieves a lower GDP, also known as the *actual GDP.* The production possibilities of a society are shown graphically using the *production possibility curve* that shows the maximum combinations of two goods that can be produced with given resources. Economic growth is portrayed by an outward shift of the *production possibility curve.*

Economic growth permeates the entire economy because all economic activity is interrelated. Indeed, households and firms are linked to each other through trade in the product and factor markets. There is a *circular flow of economic activity* as the money earned by businesses in the product market is used to pay for factors of production hired in the factor market.

In turn, the income earned by households, which are the providers of the factors of production, is used to purchase goods and services in the product market.

Any change in economic activity will work its way through the circular flow of economic activity, affecting households and firms. That initial change will result in an even greater change in the national economy; in other words, it will be magnified as it works its way through the economy in a series of consecutive cycles until completely spent. Economists call this the *multiplier process*, and the *multiplier* itself is the number by which the initial change is multiplied as it has its ultimate total effect on the economy.

SWING SHIFT

Rated PG/1984/1hr 40min/Goldie Hawn, Kurt Russell, Ed Harris
Directed by Jonathan Demme

When the men went off to war during World War II, they left a gap in the labor force. Women got recruited to take their places in factories and offices all over the United States. This film depicts the story of one couple, Jack (Ed Harris) and Kay (Goldie Hawn). When Jack enlists, Kay takes a job in the factory where he worked, the McBride Aircraft Company. Previously a homemaker, Kay suddenly finds herself earning an income, getting respect at work, and even drawing the attention of a handsome coworker, Lucky (Kurt Russell). When the war ends and Jack returns home, Kay is expected to vacate her job, together with all the other women in her position. Needless to say, the relationships between the returning husbands and their newly independent wives are fundamentally transformed.

Economic Concepts in *Swing Shift*

Scene 5 (00:00–1:17)/Minutes 12:49–14:06

After Jack goes to war, Kay is lonely and often goes to the movies by herself. On one such occasion, a government-sponsored message fills the screen before the feature begins. Its title, "Women Wanted For War Effort," is followed by a few minutes of black-and-white footage explaining how the economy needs women to enter the labor force. American men have been called into the armed forces, and women must fill their jobs. "Our boys need planes and tanks," a patriotic-sounding voice fills the theatre, "and you women can make them." Biting her lower lip in the dark theatre, Kay decides to help America win the war. She plans to embark upon a job search the very next day.

When men leave their jobs and go to war, there is a drop in economic activity because a key input has been lost. Producers cannot supply output in the absence of that input, so a drop in GDP follows. However, if their jobs are filled by replacement workers, an economic contraction need not take place. At the same time, demand in the country is increasing as additional tanks, airplanes, and military boots are needed for the war effort. Assuming the economy can hire enough inputs to produce all the demanded goods, total output will increase. The economy will therefore experience economic growth. In order to prevent a drop in supply, the government is urging women such as Kay to join the workforce.

And they do.

At the McBride Aircraft Company, dozens of women line up under the strong Santa Monica sun. Patiently they wait to be called into the employment office. One woman asks, "Are they asking for references?" Another responds, "No, you're breathing. That's good enough for them." Employers are so desperate to fill the jobs the men vacated that they are willing to hire women with minimal skills and no work experience.

Once the women start working at McBride, they not only exchange their quaint hats and white gloves for overalls, but they also become a labor input that is used to produce airplanes. Their contribution to the economy is depicted graphically as the movement from inside the production possibility curve to the curve itself. By working, the women are closing the gap between potential and actual GDP that was widened when men went to war. By increasing the supply of aircraft, these former homemakers contribute to the economic growth of the country.

Their contribution to the economy extends beyond production. By spending their wages, these women become consumers. With their expenditure on vacuum cleaners, novels, and ice cream, working women stimulate further production of those goods (as well as others).

Therefore, through production and consumption, women like Kay become part of the circular flow of economic activity. They sell their labor in the factor market in exchange for wages. They then use those wages to purchase goods and services in the product market in exchange for payment to the producers.

Discussion Questions

1. Patriotism is often invoked to change economic behavior. Some American businesses have sponsored a *Buy American* campaign that urges consumers to buy domestic goods instead of imports (for example, buy a car from Detroit rather than Japan; buy shoes from Pennsylvania rather than Italy). Comment: If all consumers bought into the *Buy American* campaign, America's economy would become stronger.

2. A large constraint facing women who want to enter the labor force is the lack of adequate child care. During World War II, this obstacle was eliminated when the government sponsored daycare centers to enable women to work. When the war ended, the daycare centers were closed. Use the concept of the multiplier to explain the effect of the opening and closing of daycare centers on women's participation in the economy.

3. All the women who waited in line at McBride's employment office got hired and spent the war years employed. When the war ended, the men returned and took back their jobs. How did this affect the GDP and the production possibility curve?

MAJOR BARBARA

By George Bernard Shaw
Mineola, NY: Dover Publications, 2002

Andrew Undershaft made a lot of money in his arms business. Yet, not one of his three children wants to have anything to do with him or his enterprise. While two are happy just living off his wealth, daughter Barbara is repelled by what her father does and in protest, becomes a major in the Salvation Army. She is passionate and committed to improving the lives of the poor and spends her days providing them with food and shelter. At the root of her disagreement with her father is the philosophical question of who does more good for society—she, by providing handouts or he, by providing employment. At the end when the Salvation Army faces closure, it is the arms industry that comes to the rescue.

Economic Concepts in *Major Barbara*

pp. 63–64

It is just before the outbreak of World War I. Andrew Undershaft's estranged daughter Barbara has agreed to visit her father in Percivale St. Andrews, the town where his armaments factory is located. She has heard that Undershaft has built up the town surrounding the factory and that he provides a decent life for his workers. Skeptical, Barbara wants to see for herself what that life looks like.

Barbara is accompanied by her brother Stephen. Together they walk through the entire town, poking around everywhere in order to find something negative—some sign that their father is exploiting his workers and not providing for them as he claims to be. But try and try, they cannot find anything wrong. Percivale St. Andrews is a quaint town in a lush valley. They are amazed at its neatly lined trees and its overall cleanliness.

How can the houses be so white when coal is used for energy, just like in London where all the buildings are discolored by it? Barbara and Stephen come across libraries, schools, clinics, and even a nursing home. By snooping around, they learn that the town hall provides a ballroom and a banquet room for the town population. Speaking to random people, Barbara and Stephen are told that Percivale St. Andrews offers its inhabitants more than physical infrastructure. The inhabitants also receive insurance from a local insurance fund, pensions from a local pension fund, and mortgages from a local bank.

At the conclusion of her excursion, Barbara has to come to terms with the fact that her father's armaments factory provides employment for its workers and therefore also an income. The lucrative arms business is able to offer its workers and their families comprehensive services that improve their quality of living. The benefits they receive range from primary education to old-age security. Barbara is reluctantly becoming convinced that the armaments factory, distasteful as it may be, does more sustained and long-term good for a larger number of people than her Salvation Army activities. Indeed, giving a poor person a meal undoubtedly has an enormous short-term benefit, but giving a poor person a job enables him to provide meals for himself and therefore has a long-term benefit.

The economic benefits of the armaments business spill beyond the city limits of Percivale St. Andrews. When workers are employed at the factory, they become part of the circular flow of economic activity. They offer their labor in the factor market, and the armaments factory employs them in exchange for wages. With their income they buy goods and services in the national product markets. By way of the multiplier effect, their consumptive expenditures on shoes, soap, and books work their way through the economy in secondary and tertiary rounds of economic activity.

Just when Barbara and Stephen stop under the shade of a tree to discuss and reevaluate their father's contribution to society, Undershaft emerges from his nearby office. Beads of perspiration form on his brow as he hurries towards his children, waving a telegram in his boney hand. Breathlessly he explains that it contains good news from China (where a war with Japan is raging). "What, another Japanese victory?" Stephen asks. Undershaft explains that he does not take sides in the faraway war. He does not care which side wins or loses. All he cares about is that both sides in the conflict buy his product. The good news he reports is that a new weapon his factory produced and exported was just put to trial for the first time and it was hugely successful—it hit a fort with three hundred soldiers and wiped them all out instantaneously.

While joy at such an outcome might seem inhumane, it is a fact that the successful performance of the new weapon will boost the factory's sales.

Those increased sales will ripple through the economy by way of the multiplier effect. They will represent an expansion of England's GDP and will contribute to economic growth throughout the country. They will also contribute to Barbara's confusion about the role her father plays in improving the lives of the poor at the cost of more efficient killing of soldiers in a far-off war.

Discussion Questions

1. According to *Major Barbara*, the war between Japan and China is good for the English economy. Apply the same reasoning to argue that the war in Iraq is good for the American economy.
2. Why is the net economic impact of a war fought *inside* a country often negative?
3. Undershaft provides his workers with a nursing home, a library, and a school. It is not clear if the workers are required to pay for those services. What is the difference in GDP if workers pay or if the services are entirely subsidized by Undershaft? Also, why is Undershaft spending his profits this way? What choices or decisions is he making?

Chapter 20

Business Cycle

Film: *CINDERELLA MAN*
Fiction: *THE GRAPES OF WRATH*

KEY ECONOMIC CONCEPTS

Economic growth is not constant. Economies sometimes expand (GDP goes up) and then at other times contract (GDP goes down). Alternating periods of economic *expansion* and *contraction* are called the *business cycle*.

A *recession* is a period of contraction in economic activity characterized by a drop in production, income, and employment. When a recession is severe and prolonged, it becomes a *depression*.

In the United States, the most severe depression happened in the early 1930s and has come to be called the *Great Depression*. It involved a stock market crash, a trade war, and a banking crisis. As a result, many firms went out of business and had to lay off workers. Real GDP went down by 27 percent during 1929–1933, and unemployment reached 25 percent in 1933.

CINDERELLA MAN

Rated PG-13/2005/2hr 25 min/Russell Crowe, Renée Zellweger
Directed by Ron Howard

Jim Braddock (Russell Crowe) is a boxer in New Jersey when the Great Depression starts. His flagging career comes to an end when hard times force him to leave the ring and take on a series of menial jobs in order to feed his family. Jim and his wife Mae (Renée Zellweger) are thrilled when he gets a job at a shipyard and has a steady income. However, he soon injures his hand and has to give up his dream of boxing in the future. Then one day, due to a last minute cancellation, he is invited to box with a champion. He takes this opportunity, despite his injury. Although everyone believes he cannot possibly beat Max Baer, Braddock succeeds in making one of the greatest upsets in boxing history. This film is based on real events.

Economic Concepts in *Cinderella Man*

Scene 2 (0:42–5:22)/ Minutes 8:40–13:20

It is four years into the Great Depression, and Jim and Mae have moved from their large home into a one-room rental. Together with their three children, they sleep, cook, and eat in a single room. They are the lucky ones. Outside their building, the street is filled with makeshift tents where families live, heated only by the occasional fire burning in a nearby steel container.

One scene in *Cinderella Man* illustrates the repercussions of economic contraction. It begins when Jim gets up in the morning while it is still dark, hoping to get a head start on his job search. Jim is unemployed, along with millions of other Americans. He is not looking for a full-time job that pays a good salary and includes benefits. Such a goal is much too ambitious for the times. Jim is merely looking for a day's wage with which to buy a few groceries for his kids. Unemployment such as Jim's is common at low points of the business cycle.

Jim dresses in partial darkness. His family now uses only one low wattage light bulb to save electricity. His only pair of socks gets washed at night and dried in the oven as multiple clothes have become a luxury. It is cold in the room as heating is too expensive to use continuously. Mae has adjusted to this by wearing a sweater at all times. When young Rosie wakes up with hunger pains, Mae places a lone piece of spam on her plate. She gobbles it up and asks for more, whimpering that she is still hungry. In a selfless fatherly gesture, Jim transfers his own thin slice onto her plate, assuring her that he is still full from his dream in which he ate steak, mashed potatoes, and ice cream with Mickey Rooney at the Ritz. When Jim steps outside to pick up the milk bottle (in those days milkmen filled and left bottles outside front doors), he finds a past due notice next to an unfilled bottle. No money, no milk. But Mae is resourceful—she adds water to the one inch of milk left over in the fridge, thereby tricking five stomachs into thinking they've been fed. These are just some of the ways in which Jim's family experienced poverty. They are indicators of a downturn in the business cycle and a decrease in the GDP per capita.

When he leaves home that morning, Jim proceeds to the shipyard where throngs of men hover in the cold, hoping to be picked for manual labor. The cigarettes hanging from their lips provide the only pleasure most will have that day. When a manager approaches them to choose a handful of men, the throng moves up around the wrought iron fence, a compressed body of humanity with multiple arms jutting out, imploring "Pick me! Pick me!" The manager's woolen coat and gentleman's hat stand in sharp contrast to the destitute laborers as he calls out, "You!" and "You there!" and "You, yes you!" until he reaches nine. After that, in a dismissive tone he tells the others to disperse. Those others represent potential workers and potential output. Hiring them would have closed the gap between potential GDP and actual GDP.

Discussion Questions

1. Braddock was called the Cinderella Man because his story, like that of Cinderella (in the fairy tale), has a happy ending. Using economic concepts you have learned to date, explain how else their experiences are similar.
2. Assume the shipyard hires eighteen men for a half day each instead of nine men for a whole day. What is the effect on the shipyard's total payroll? What is the effect on the living conditions of the eighteen men? What are the possible effects on total labor output?
3. Given Jim's unemployment, Mae has a pent-up demand for numerous household items such as cleaning supplies, lightbulbs, and children's shoes. When Jim begins to earn, Mae immediately spends part of his income on those items. Pick one and describe how her purchase would work its way through the economy, contributing to an upward swing of the business cycle.

THE GRAPES OF WRATH

By John Steinbeck (winner of 1962 Nobel Prize in Literature)
New York: Penguin, 2002

The Joads are a family of Oklahoma farmers who are experiencing all the pain of the Depression. Because of a drought, their crops have failed and they cannot make debt payments to their bank. As a result, they are evicted from the land and become migrant workers. They work their way to California, together with many others in their situation. The journey is filled with heart-wrenching problems; hunger, bad weather, and death are their constant companions. Even when the Joads finally arrive at their destination, their problems continue as they are not welcomed by the locals.

Economic Concepts in *The Grapes of Wrath*

pp. 31–32

At the turn of the twentieth century, many farming families in rural Oklahoma were too poor to own land. They were tenants, leasing land from landowners whom they paid with a hefty share of their crop. In the years when they had a bad crop, these tenants typically borrowed money from a bank in order to make their payments (and put food on the table). This tenant system was strained by the economic downturn of the Great Depression. However, it was a severe drought and a series of ferocious dust storms (known as the Dust Bowl) that caused major agricultural damage and ultimately felled the tenant system.

In *The Grapes of Wrath*, the Joad family huddles behind closed doors as dust sweeps across the plains and seeps into their house and their lungs. They had always relied on rain to irrigate their crops as they were too poor to invest in a more reliable irrigation system. Now, in the absence of rain, they watch the land become dry and brittle. Cracks form in the soil, and crops shrivel and die. Bending down to touch the soil, Mr. Joad knows all its life has disappeared, and without life, there is no output. Unable to make their sharecropping payments to their landlord, who in this case is the local bank, the Joads took out several consecutive loans, always expecting their luck to turn. It didn't, and one day bank representatives show up at their door to repossess the land.

The two men, with hats pulled low over their eyes, do not even bother to get out of the black sedan when they inform Mr. Joad he has to vacate his home. The bank has arranged the demolition of the house to take place the next day. In this matter-of-fact way, the Joads are given twenty-four hours to salvage their belongings before the bulldozers arrive.

To add insult to injury, the two men then explain how all the farmers are to be replaced by tractors. Mechanization of agriculture is the way of the future since one man on a tractor can do the work of a dozen tenant families. That man will be paid a wage, and the owner will take the entire crop. For the bank, it is a far less complicated system of agricultural production than sharecropping.

Mr. Joad pleads with them, telling them he has no place to go, nothing to do. He has no savings. He has no skills other than farming.

Paid work is hard to find in an economic downturn. Producers are not hiring workers. They do not need them because they have reduced their output in response to the drop in demand for goods and services. People across the country have less money to make purchases. National output and employment are on a downward spiral.

Mr. Joad knows all this, and his desperation is palpable. His raggedy kids stand in the sun-beaten yard, drawing random formations with sticks in the dust. They wait.

After a long and painful silence, the bank spokesmen tell the Joads to go out west. And they do, becoming part of some four hundred thousand residents of Oklahoma and other Plains states who moved west in search of work during the 1930s in what became known as the Dust Bowl Migration.

Unemployment and poverty stayed with the Joad family even after they reached California. The economy did not begin the upward swing of the business cycle until many years alter.

Discussion Questions

1. In *The Grapes of Wrath*, banks foreclose on tenants' properties because tenants cannot make their payments. Comment: It is 2008 and since many banks are foreclosing on American homeowners who cannot make their monthly mortgage payments, it must mean that the economy is in a depression.

2. During the Great Depression, tenants became unemployed not only because of the contracting economy but also because of mechanization. In *The Grapes of Wrath*, Mr. Joad learns that he and his fellow tenants are to be replaced by tractors. Why would a bank make such capital investments during an economic downturn? What would be the effects of such investment on the GDP?

3. Bad weather affects the economy. This was true in Oklahoma during the 1930s, and it was true in New Orleans after Hurricane Katrina (2005). The regional economy in New Orleans went into a recession. Which economic indicators do you think were affected following the hurricane, and how?

Chapter 21

Capital and Investment

Film: *BARBARIANS AT THE GATE*
Fiction: *THE MERCHANT OF VENICE*

KEY ECONOMIC CONCEPTS

Economic growth and the upswing of the business cycle are often accompanied by *investment*. Investment refers to spending by firms. Firms invest in order to expand operations by spending on new plants and equipment. Investment also includes changes in the firms' inventories.

In order to invest, firms need money. They have two sources of funds—internal and external. *Internal financing* refers to the use of financial sources within the company. Mostly that refers to reinvesting a part of the firm's profits (called *retained earnings*). It also includes bringing other partners into the firm who come with their own resources to invest.

External financing occurs when firms turn to sources of money outside of their company. They can acquire funding directly from borrowers through financial markets. The two most common types of such *direct financing* include stocks and bonds. *Stocks* are financial securities that indicate ownership of a firm. *Dividends* are payments that a corporation pays to its shareholders out of the firms' profits. If a firm does not want to give out ownership rights but just wants to borrow money, then it can issue bonds. *Bonds* are financial securities that represent a loan—a promise to repay a certain amount of money. Firms raise money by issuing bonds that promise to pay interest (called a *coupon payment*) as well as the principal at the end of the bond's term.

Alternatively, firms can acquire funding indirectly through financial intermediaries, most commonly banks that transfer money from savers to borrowers (*indirect financing*). The way banks function is described in chapter 28.

The *interest rate* is the cost of borrowing money for investment spending. It is important in determining the quantity of investment spending that businesses undertake. Considered the price of money, the interest rate is inversely related to investment by the law of demand (the higher the interest rate, the fewer funds will be borrowed for investment).

The interest rate is also important for households that supply savings. *Savings* refer to the after-tax income that is not consumed. Savings are usually kept in interest-bearing accounts that are governed by the law of supply: the higher the interest rate, the more money households save. Through the financial system those savings translate into funds for firms to borrow (see chapter 28 for additional information on banking).

In economics, the term capital usually refers to *physical capital* and includes goods that are used to produce other goods, such as machinery, tools, and equipment. *Financial capital* consists of stocks, bank accounts, and other holdings of money.

BARBARIANS AT THE GATE

Rated R/1993/1hr 47min/James Garner, Jonathan Pryce
Directed by Glenn Jordan

This film is based on real events involved in the RJR-Nabisco buyout that took place in the 1980s. Ross Johnson (James Garner) is the company CEO who makes a bid to buy the conglomerate and in the process to make a fortune for himself. He expects the sale to be easy but underestimates the greed of others who, like him, are seeking to make fortunes and build reputations. Henry Kravis (Jonathan Pryce) becomes the strongest competitor, and Wall Street becomes the stage where the two men engage in battle.

Economic Concepts in *Barbarians at the Gate*

Scene 7 (4:22–5:12)/Minutes 27:43–28:33

Ross and his wife fly their private plane to Connecticut where they have been invited to lunch at the estate of old friends, Jim and Linda. They sit down to a meal on the patio of a huge Tudor-style mansion surrounded by walls of thick ivy. The table is set with care, probably by the same housekeeper who earlier was seen ironing dollar bills to make them as perfect as everything else in the house. The powerful men and their well-maintained wives engage in friendly chitchat across the begonia centerpiece until Ross introduces the subject he came to discuss: the buyout of RJR Nabisco. Since Jim is the chairman of American Express, Ross wants him to organize the buyout.

In order to buy the company, Ross needs financial capital, not physical capital. He is looking for external indirect financing, and Jim assures him that Shearson Lehman, a division of American Express, can and will raise the money he needs. Shearson is headed by Peter Cohen who, incidentally, has never done a buyout of this size before. Jim is quick to add that Peter's inexperience poses no problem as he simply needs to follow the usual procedures for a buyout. In the case of Nabisco, those procedures include the following. First Ross must state what he wants for himself in the deal. Then he has to make the company records available to the Shearson team. Peter and his people will then go to work and come up with a proper bid for Ross to make. It is a simple plan, laid out between sips of orange juice from Jim's crystal glass.

Is the buyout a good idea? RJR Nabisco is not doing well, and its stock is valued at an all-time low. As the CEO, Ross is motivated to save the company (as well as his lavish lifestyle). When in an earlier scene Ross first mentioned his intended buyout to a friend, the response he got was, "Don't do it. It's like cutting off your arm to get rid of a hangnail." That friend was risk averse and clearly concerned about raising a lot of money (that is, taking on debt) for a company so poorly valued.

By contrast, Jim is not risk averse. Rather than trying to talk his friend out of the buyout, Jim is thrilled Ross chose his company to raise the necessary capital. He is blinded by the expected income sure to come his way. Indeed, Shearson Lehman/American Express will raise big money and therefore will extract a big payment. Expected earnings are large enough that when Jim calls Peter to announce Ross chose them to arrange the buyout, he says, "Cancel your life for the next few weeks." The opportunity cost of putting a highly paid employee such as Peter on an exclusive assignment for three weeks is undoubtedly very high. Jim knows it, and Peter knows it. That is why, when they speak by phone, one at lunch in Connecticut and the other on a California tennis court, they both smile into their oversized 1980s cell phones. Their facial expressions reflect unadulterated greed.

Greed makes all players in the Nabisco deal take risks. Ross seals the deal with Jim and proceeds with the buyout plans. All this takes place over the main course on Jim's patio.

Later, over dessert and coffee, Linda raises the question of privacy, urging Ross to be secretive about the deal lest he have a feeding frenzy on his hands. Indeed, she says everyone ("and his brother," Jim adds for emphasis) will try to buy up the company. Ross smiles—of course he thought about the privacy issue. That's why he wants to have the bid ready to spring to the board at its next meeting, in three weeks time. As long as there is a lid on purchase preparations, others will not have time to prepare their bids.

In the midst of this conversation about secrecy, gunshots are heard. Ross and his wife look up in wonder. Linda assures them there is nothing amiss, just their neighbor hunting quail. That neighbor happens to be Henry Kravis, a wealthy banker who soon ends up being Ross's biggest competitor. The shots portend the soon-to-begin battle between the two Wall Street giants.

Discussion Questions

1. How is a student loan an example of external financing for investment? What is the investment? What other source of funding do students have at their disposal?
2. Using some key concepts, tell the Nabisco Board of Directors what Ross is trying to do.
3. In 2006, basketball star Shaquille O'Neil opened a fitness center in Miami (*Coconut Grove Shaq Club*). Surely he had enough personal savings to invest in his enterprise; yet, it is likely that he used borrowed funds. What can you infer about the interest rate on his loan relative to the expected rate of return on his invested assets?

THE MERCHANT OF VENICE

By William Shakespeare
New York: Washington Square Press, 1992

This play takes place during the Middle Ages in Venice, which at the time was a rich republic with a highly developed maritime industry. Young Bassanio asks his more established friend Antonio to lend him money (3,000 ducats) in order to court the beautiful Portia. Antonio is happy to oblige but since all his money is tied up in ships currently at sea, he needs to borrow the money. He approaches Shylock the moneylender. They agree on a loan with interesting terms: a pound of flesh is to be extracted from Antonio if he defaults on his loan by the repayment date. As it turns out, Antonio's ships are lost at sea, and he cannot make the payments on time. Although Shylock demands his perverse payment, Portia's impersonation of a legal expert turns the contract upside down to Shylock's detriment, who suffers greatly as a result.

Economic Concepts in *The Merchant of Venice*

pp. 29–30

Shylock is the most prominent moneylender in the Republic of Venice. He lends money to anybody who wants it, for any reason. In exchange, he charges a fee. In Shakespearean times that fee was called the "rate of usance" while today it is known as the interest rate. Although lending money to individuals and businesses is an integral part of contemporary banking, it was not so in medieval Europe. The existing financial system was inadequate. It did not satisfy the demand for financial capital for investment nor the demand for personal expenditure. In addition, stocks and bonds as we now know them did not exist.

Shylock is about to meet with Antonio to discuss his upcoming loan. It is clear that Shylock does not like Antonio. While there are many reasons for their mutual antipathy, Shylock's dislike is primarily rooted in Antonio's financial activities. Those activities are indirectly undermining Shylock's business.

Antonio often lends money to a variety of individuals but, unlike Shylock, he charges no interest. Antonio is viewed as the preferred source of loans by anyone who seeks to borrow money. He offers a substitute to Shylock's money. As a result of his loans, there is a drop in demand for Shylock's (more expensive) loans. Such a decrease in demand results in a lower equilibrium price of money (interest rate) that moneylenders can charge in the money market. Thus, the financial service industry in Venice is affected by Antonio's behavior, as are Shylock's earnings.

Shylock also dislikes Antonio because he publicly insulted Shylock for always being on the lookout for "bargains" and for having a predisposition for "thrift." Antonio's description of Shylock's behavior illustrates how views of finance have changed over time. In contemporary economies, seeking out bargains is viewed as rational behavior while being thrifty is associated with increased savings, which in turn are associated with investment and financing. Far from being insults, today such characteristics are complimentary.

Incidentally, Antonio incurs an opportunity cost every time he makes a loan without charging interest. That cost is the amount of interest he has given up. Antonio has both the ability and the incentive to consistently incur such opportunity costs. He is wealthy (that gives him ability), and he wants to ingratiate himself with the Venetian population for social and political purposes (that provides the incentive).

In *The Merchant of Venice*, Shylock refers to the place where merchants congregate. It is a particular square in Venice where people come together to make deals that involve buying and selling of financial capital. There is no such physical meeting place in complex modern economies. Rather, the buying and selling of financial capital takes place in the financial markets, including the stock market, the bond market, banks, and others.

Discussion Questions

1. In *The Merchant of Venice*, Bassanio borrows money for romantic purposes. What are some contemporary examples of borrowing money (and paying interest) for romantic purposes?
2. Comment: There is no difference between the central square in Venice and New York's Wall Street when it comes to buying and selling of financial capital.
3. In a later scene, Shylock agrees to lend Antonio money but, because he doesn't like him, he stipulates that loan delinquency requires payment with a pound of flesh. How could he have instead used standard financial tools to show his antipathy for Antonio?

Chapter 22

Human Capital

Film: *BORN YESTERDAY*
Fiction: *THE SWORD IN THE STONE*

KEY ECONOMIC CONCEPTS

In addition to physical and financial capital, human capital is also crucial for the functioning and growth of an economy. *Human capital* refers to the accumulation of skills and knowledge that workers get from education and on-the-job training. The quantity of human capital in a society determines its *labor productivity*. The more *skills* and education a worker has, the more productive he or she is.

One of the most fundamental skills that workers have is literacy. *Literacy* refers to reading and writing at a level that enables communication with others and so allows individuals to participate more fully in society. Since increased literacy tends to be associated with enhanced thinking skills, employers prefer to hire literate people even for work that does not specifically require reading or writing.

BORN YESTERDAY

Rated PG/1993/1hr 40 min/ Melanie Griffith, John Goodman, Don Johnson
Directed by Luis Mandoki

Harry Brock (John Goodman) has made a fortune in real estate. He goes to Washington for an extended trip in order to lobby some senators to vote in his favor: namely, against the closing of a military base next door to his shopping mall. The problem is his seemingly silly girlfriend Billie (Melanie Griffith) who always says the wrong thing and embarrasses him. Brock wishes she were a little more educated, so he hires a journalist, Paul Vernon (Don Johnson), to teach Billie some basics to stop her from being a liability. Billie responds very well to education and soon learns not only classical literature but also about Brock's illegal business affairs. In the end, Brock wishes he had never brought her to Washington.

Economic Concepts in *Born Yesterday*

Scene 4 (0:00–1:40)/ Minutes 25:47–27:28

Soon after Harry and Billie move to Washington, Billie is asked to appear on a radio station. On the show, she is herself—beautiful, enthusiastic, and innocently silly. She makes several foolish statements, showing millions of listeners how uneducated she is. Under the probing of a malicious reporter, Billie makes a fool of herself and, by extension, of Harry. Horrified by her words and the ensuing commentary, Harry's legal advisor insists that Billie be sent home. In his view, Billie doesn't know anything about anything and must be muzzled, or else she will undermine Harry's lobbying efforts in Washington. She has already become a liability.

Harry mulls over his predicament. When he met Billie in Las Vegas years ago, she seemed smart enough. But now, in Washington, she seems "downright stupid." In other words, the skills Billie used in Vegas are not relevant for the job she performs in Washington. The employment requirements are different in the two cities. In Vegas she was a hostess, a job that required her to be attractive, wear revealing clothes, and communicate with a soothing voice. There was no need to speak intelligently or have a broad range of knowledge. By contrast, Billie's "job" in Washington is to be a presentable companion to a man who is trying to make a good impression on the country's political leaders. Never having been in that job before, Billie had no opportunity to acquire appropriate skills.

Billie now needs on-the-job training. If she does not receive it, Harry (her de facto boss) has two alternatives: he can fire her because she cannot perform the job she was brought to Washington to perform (that is, he can send her home), or he can undergo the expense of training her (namely, skill acquisition in the workplace).

Harry is a shrewd businessman, used to getting what he wants. He wants Billie at his side, but he also wants her to appear more educated so as not to embarrass him. He proposes to "smarten her up." All Billie needs is the right learning environment and/or the right person to teach her, he says. Since it is too late to send her to school, Harry has a different idea: intensive one-to-one training.

In support of this idea, Harry tells his skeptical adviser that Billie is a quick study. For example, she didn't know how to play gin rummy when they met and then once he taught her, she beat him every time they played.

In pursuit of his goal, Harry calls Paul Vernon, a reporter who also teaches at Georgetown. They meet for a power lunch in a Washington restaurant filled with men in suits. There they agree on a price of $500 per day to "smarten Billie up." But Harry fails to consider all possible outcomes of his gamble. He does not consider, for example, that an educated Billie will know how to think logically, express herself eloquently, and read with understanding. As such, she will represent an addition to society's stock of human capital. The education she will get from Vernon will soon make her overeducated for Harry's gin rummy games. She will be able to supply her new skills in the labor market and aim at higher-paying jobs than she had before. She might even decide to leave Harry.

Discussion Questions

1. Why are you pursuing a higher education? What are the benefits to you? What are the benefits to society?
2. Using key concepts, explain how summer internships impact students' future job searches.
3. Harry was insightful (and somewhat crude) when he said that Billie's skills were successful in Las Vegas and inadequate in Washington. Apply this idea of appropriate skills to an electrical engineer who took a job teaching kids to swim. Identify which skills are transferable and which are irrelevant in his new position.

THE SWORD IN THE STONE

By T. H. White
New York: Bantam Doubleday Dell, 1963

This is the story of King Arthur when he was a child in medieval England. Arthur was not born in the high courts. Rather, he was Sir Ector's ward and ran errands around the castle. Everyone called him the Wart. One day

Arthur meets Merlyn the magician and his talking owl Archimedes. Merlyn knows Arthur will become the future king of England, so he begins to train him for the job. Not only does Arthur learn how to hunt and use the sword, but more importantly he also learns how to think. When Merlyn finally decides that Arthur is ready, the stage is set for the famous sword-in-the-stone scene: whoever can pull the sword out of the stone will be the rightful king of England. Of course, it is Arthur who succeeds.

Economic Concepts in *The Sword in the Stone*

pp. 51–52

On a hot August day, Merlyn leads Arthur outdoors for a lesson in experience.

The skinny boy and his new mentor cross the bridge over the moat surrounding Sir Ector's castle. Arthur dreamily looks towards the water and says, I wish I were a fish. Whether he meant it or not is irrelevant to Merlyn, who recognizes an opportunity for a life lesson and jumps to oblige. With a few magic words (*Snylrem stnemilpmoc ot enutpen dna lliw eh yldnik tpecca siht yob sa a hsif*) and a midair twirl of his elongated staff, Merlyn turns Arthur into a fish. Moments later, Arthur is naked, splashing around in a moat that grows bigger and bigger by the moment. Soon it is a vast sea, and Arthur is a scaly fish with fins and a tail.

Merlyn calls out to him, explaining the reason for the magical transformation. In his role as teacher, Merlyn seeks to provide learning experiences for Arthur. Merlyn wants to expose him to a broad range of opportunities aimed at widening his horizons and teaching him about the world. Experiences, Merlyn believes, are education. They provide training no less real than that found in books. Unbeknownst to Arthur, Merlyn is trying to prepare him for his future role as king. Learning what it is like to be a fish will be useful when he needs to put himself in the state of mind of his subjects and consider a broad range of interests in his kingdom. Accumulated experiences will enable him to become a more effective ruler.

Merlyn also wants to teach Arthur self-reliance, and the water experience will undoubtedly do that. Indeed, when Arthur first falls into the moat and becomes a fish, he tries to swim like a human being. Those strokes and motions do not get him very far as they are not appropriate for a fish's body. It is only when, through trial and error, Arthur puts himself into the state of mind of another being that he figures out how to swim like a fish. No one does it for him; he has to rely on himself.

After that summer day, Arthur continues to receive an education although he does not go to school nor does he study with peers. Instead, he gets one-on-one lessons from Merlyn in whatever subject the magician sees fit to teach, whenever he feels like teaching. Sometimes the lessons take place at a desk when Arthur reads about science and solves math problems. At other times, Merlyn takes him deep into the woods so Arthur can learn how to hunt and use a sword. All that knowledge is ultimately an addition to England's stock of human capital.

As it turns out, after Arthur becomes king of England, he remembers the value of all he learned with Merlyn and strives to promote education among his subjects.

Discussion Questions

1. Comment: A liberal arts education for American students is like learning to swim like a fish was for Arthur.

2. Merlin believed it was important for medieval leaders to be educated. Is such education also important in the twenty-first century? Why are voters concerned with the educational credentials of their presidential candidates?

3. Comment: If experiences contribute to my education, then why are my parents opposed to my partying experiences?

Chapter 23

Entrepreneurs

Film: *CHARLIE AND THE CHOCOLATE FACTORY*
Fiction: *CATCH-22*

KEY ECONOMIC CONCEPTS

Evidence from across the globe has shown that countries where entrepreneurship is vibrant tend to have more economic growth. *Entrepreneurs* are the individuals who start and operate businesses. They have an idea about an economic activity, and they put it into practice. In so doing, they bring together labor, capital, and other resources. They are *risk-takers*, often investing their own funds in their business. Their ideas are often *innovative* so their investments contribute to economic progress. Without entrepreneurs, technological change in a society would be much slower.

CHARLIE AND THE CHOCOLATE FACTORY

Rated PG/2005/1hr 55 min/Johnny Depp, Freddie Highmore, David Kelly
Directed by Tim Burton

Willy Wonka (Johnny Depp) owns the biggest chocolate factory in the globe. His chocolates and candies are sold all over the world. For fifteen years no one has been inside the factory, and no one knows how his chocolates are made. One day Willy invites five children to spend a day inside the factory, the five who find a golden ticket in their chocolate bar wrapping. A global frenzy ensues. One of the five children turns out to be Charlie Buckett (Freddie Highmore). He grew up on stories about Willy Wonka from his Grandpa Joe (David Kelly) who worked in the factory some twenty years ago. The day Charlie spends inside the chocolate factory changes his life forever as he learns many important life lessons.

Economic Concepts in *Charlie and the Chocolate Factory*

Scene 2 (1:55–3:06)/ Minutes 6:08–7:19
Scene 4 (0:00–1:19)/ Minutes 9:52–11:11

Charlie lives in a shack with his parents and two sets of grandparents. They are so poor that they eat cabbage with cabbage every night for dinner. Afterwards, they huddle together, sharing a blanket and telling stories. Grandpa Joe delights young Charlie with remembrances of his tenure in Willy Wonka's chocolate factory, when he worked on the candy assembly line. He was one of the early workers in what later became a highly profitable business that still sells Wonka chocolates all across the globe.

This huge international chocolate empire was built by one lone entrepreneur, Willy Wonka. He is an eccentric who lives by himself and devotes all his waking hours to his creative ideas. His innovations focus on new production methods, such as mixing chocolate by way of a waterfall to keep it light and frothy. Alternatively Willy's innovations introduce new products to the market. Among Grandpa Joe's favorites are chocolate-covered birds that, when placed on the tongue, produce a chirping sound. Another favorite is ice cream that stays cold for hours, even if left in the sun on a hot day.

Wonka chocolates and candies were so popular that demand overwhelmed the production capacity of the corner shop on Cherry Street. To increase supply, Willy invested in a new factory. As Grandpa Joe tells it, this was the biggest factory in history, fifty times bigger than any other in the world. On the new site, chocolates and candies and chewing gums and lollipops were produced and supplied to global markets via an intricate distribution system.

The more sweets Willy supplied, the more insatiable the demand seemed to be, leading Willy to concentrate even more on new products and production methods. Willy seemed on a never-ending trajectory of growth and success. And the benefits of his success spread across the country as technological innovation, international trade, and economic growth all flourished. Everyone was joyous at Willy's success. Well, not really everyone.

His competitors, other chocolate and candy producers, were envious. They resented Willy's good reputation, his phenomenal earnings, and his growing share of the sweets industry. Willy had cornered the candy and chocolate market while their puny shares were dwindling daily. In order to destroy him, they planted spies inside the factory. These spies were camouflaged as ordinary workers who worked side by side with loyal staff like Grandpa Joe. But they kept their eyes and ears open, stealing ideas and recipes.

Soon Fickelgruber made ice cream that didn't melt, and Prodnos came out with chewing gum that never lost its flavor. Slugwood made candy balloons that blew up to incredible sizes. Such competition put Willy Wonka's business operation at risk. Sales quickly dropped, followed by earnings. Soon the chocolate factory had to close its doors, and all the workers were let go. Grandpa Joe lost the job he loved.

But Willy Wonka was not a quitter. His entrepreneurial skills led him to a new innovative idea that enabled him to bounce back and produce even more chocolate than before. This time, no one from the town was allowed through the factory gates so that no one could steal his ideas. We learn later in the film that Willy Wonka's innovative idea had to do with changing inputs into production, which led to a change in the production function. He found a source of workers from abroad who were unlikely to spy on him.

The idea came to Willy when he was on a mission in Oompa-Loompa, searching for new exotic tastes for his candies. There he met the Oompa-Loompans, tiny jungle people who revered one thing above all: the rare cocoa bean. Willy Wonka proposed a trade. If they come work for him in his chocolate factory, Willy will pay them with cocoa beans. To the Oompa-Loompans, beans were more precious than dollars. To Willy, beans were abundant as he had years ago identified reliable and cheap suppliers. And so, a deal was made. Willy's labor costs were reduced, and his output was increased. Wonka chocolates were again sold all over the world.

As all entrepreneurs, Willy took risks. He took a risk by importing Oompa-Loompans who could have turned out to be unadaptable to the North American climate. He took a risk by introducing new products that might have unintended side effects, such as when a girl called Violet turned purple after trying the three-course-dinner gum stick. And he took the ultimate risk when he tried to identify an heir to his chocolate business.

Discussion Questions

1. Willy Wonka closed his factory door to workers when he learned that his secret recipe was stolen. In the real world, how do companies such as Coca Cola manage to keep their recipes secret? How does entrepreneurship depend on the ability to keep such secrets?

2. How did Willy Wonka's expansion from Cherry Street to the big new factory result in economic growth? Discuss two markets that were affected by his move.

3. In order to promote products, creative advertisers come up with catchy phrases such as the one Willy Wonka used: "Cavity-filling Caramels—No More Dentists." What are some catchy phrases associated with the products you purchase?

CATCH-22

By Joseph Heller
New York: Simon and Schuster, 2004

The setting for this novel is an imaginary island off the coast of Italy, during World War II. Yossarian is a bombardier for the U.S. army who desperately wants to complete his service and return home. However, his boss Colonel Cathcart keeps adding tasks that Yossarian must perform before he is given leave. The entire book is about absurd situations a group of imaginary military men get into during the war. It blurs the distinction between sanity and insanity and shows how illogical bureaucracy can be.

Economic Concepts in *Catch-22*

pp. 230–232

Yossarian and Milo are in a two-seater plane. They are returning to the base after making a few runs in Naples, Sicily, and Malta—all for war profiteering purposes. Although Milo is a sergeant in the army, he considers himself first and foremost the base's entrepreneur. The absurdity that permeates *Catch-22* is also reflected in the description of Milo's entrepreneurship abilities as well as his thinking about economic concepts.

Milo has organized an extensive and profitable business operation that involves trade in eggs. On the airplane, he explains to Yossarian how this business functions. Milo buys eggs for seven cents in Malta and then resells them for five cents in order to make a profit. When Yossarian points out that far from making a profit, Milo is losing two cents per egg, the self-confident entrepreneur disagrees and continues explaining his scheme. It turns out that Milo buys eggs in Sicily for one cent and then takes them to Malta where he sells them for seven cents. Then he buys them at seven cents and resells them on the base for five cents. Little by little, the truth is revealed. The people Milo refers to as the buyers are in fact him. In other words, Milo buys eggs from himself that he then sells to himself. Milo explains this process to Yossarian:

"I'm the people I buy them [the eggs] from," Milo explained. "I make a profit of three and a quarter cents apiece when I sell them to me and a profit of two and three quarter cents apiece when I buy them back from me."

In addition, Milo acts as his own middleman and thereby secures for himself a cut that further adds to his profits.

As Milo describes it, the success of his scheme relies on consistency of consumer behavior. He relies on people's willingness to travel to Malta to buy eggs, even if they are more expensive there, only because that is how they have always done it. He relies on their unwillingness to even try to buy eggs in Sicily because they've never done it that way. People are behaving irrationally, and Milo's business success is predicated on the continued irrationality of consumers. If one day people realize that they are buying eggs at higher prices than they need to, Milo's egg business will crumble, and he will lose the source of his profits. Of course, since Milo is "the people," he therefore controls both demand and supply and so he alone has the power to make or break his egg business. Many nonfictional entrepreneurs would like to have such market power.

Milo thinks this absurd profit-making scheme shows how entrepreneurial he is. He convinces Yossarian that his is a unique business. In fact, neither one of them has ever heard of any other entrepreneur who buys from himself and sells to himself and in the process makes profits. To the extent that entrepreneurship refers to the application of innovative ideas to the market place, Milo is certainly an entrepreneur.

Discussion Questions

1. Milo is not the only entrepreneur in the egg business. Outside of fiction, two innovative ideas stand out for their creativity. One such idea entails molding eggshells into square shapes for easier packaging (and therefore less breakage during transport). Another idea entails artificially shortening the day and night cycle according to which hens lay eggs, thereby tricking hens into doubling their egg output. If successful, how would these two entrepreneurial ideas affect the GDP?
2. In 1990, the international community imposed sanctions on Iraq, curtailing its ability to trade (in hopes of modifying its political behavior). Some entrepreneurial individuals saw sanctions as an opportunity for new creative ways of conducting illegal trade (this is called sanction-busting). The existence of such war profiteers shows that entrepreneurial activity is not necessarily good for society. Who benefits from war profiteering? How do the risks of sanction-busting compare to expected profits?
3. Entrepreneurs bring together resources to put their innovative ideas into practice for an economic activity. Which resources does Milo bring together in his egg business, and what is his innovative idea?

Chapter 24

Inflation

Film: *THE WEDDING SINGER*
Fiction:
A CONNECTICUT YANKEE IN KING ARTHUR'S COURT

KEY ECONOMIC CONCEPTS

Prices of goods and services are not fixed over time. When the average level of prices in a society rises, economists call it *inflation;* when it falls, it is *deflation*. One way to measure inflation is by using the *consumer price index* (CPI) that monitors average prices in a *basket of commodities* purchased by a typical family.

There are many reasons why inflation occurs. It can happen when there is too much demand relative to the existing supply; in other words, when there is too much money chasing too few goods (*demand pull inflation*). Inflation also happens when increases in the cost of production decrease the supply of goods relative to their demand (*cost push inflation*). Inflation is also passed from one country to another when countries engage in trade (*international transmission of inflation).*

Economists distinguish between nominal prices and real prices of goods, services, and resources. The *nominal price* refers to the price paid at the final purchase point of sale while the *real price* is that price adjusted for inflation. In other words, the difference between these prices is inflation. Real prices are adjusted for inflation while nominal prices are not.

When inflation occurs, prices of goods as well as factors of production are affected. A *wage and price spiral* occurs when workers demand higher wages to offset the increased prices of goods that they buy. That prompts firms to raise prices of goods in order to offset the increased wages they must pay their workers. The adjustment of a worker's wage, to compensate for inflation, is called the *cost of living adjustment*.

THE WEDDING SINGER

Rated PG-13/1998/1 hr 35 min/Adam Sandler, Drew Barrymore
Directed by Frank Coraci

Robbie Hart (Adam Sandler) is a wedding singer. He likes his work, even if it doesn't pay well. However, his girlfriend is embarrassed by his job and walks out on him on their wedding day. Robbie becomes unhappy and angry, putting his own job in peril, as it requires faking happiness that he is unable to do. Julia Sullivan (Drew Barrymore) comes to the rescue. She is a waitress that works at the weddings where Robbie sings. They become friends. Julia is about to marry Glenn, a selfish Wall Street banker, but breaks off the relationship when she realizes that she loves Robbie.

Economic Concepts in *The Wedding Singer*

Scene 13 (2:54–3:09)/ Minutes 54:45–55:01

Julia and her roommate Holly (Christine Taylor) are sitting in their kitchen discussing Julia's upcoming wedding. Glenn walks in, carrying a cardboard box with bold Sony labels. His muscular arms are strained from the weight. He proudly announces that he bought Julia a present: a CD player. It is a new product on the market—so new that Julia thinks it plays records. She has never heard of CDs. Glenn takes on a macho professorial tone as he teaches her about the new machine. First he focuses on the sound it produces. "It is outstanding," he purrs. Then he adds a shocking piece of news. Its price tag is $700.

This price information clearly dates the *Wedding Singer*. At present, CD players can typically be purchased for some $200, representing a sharp decrease over their price just one decade earlier. As many other goods affected by rapid technological change, CD players have decreased in price since their introduction to the market. In other words, they have experienced price deflation. Televisions, computers, photographic equipment, and calculators, like CD players, have thus become more affordable. At the same time, their quality has also improved. Undoubtedly, the sound on state-of-the-art music players is higher today than it was a decade ago, when Glenn surprised Julia with a Sony.

Given that the price has dropped due to technological change, the ensuing deflation might be called "cost-push deflation" insofar as improved technology results in lower costs of production that stimulate increases in supply. Greater supply leads to lower equilibrium prices.

Other items in Julia's apartment, such as the floral sofa, the exercise bicycle, and the Kenmore fridge, have all become more expensive over the past decade. The fact that a typical bundle of commodities contains items whose prices have decreased, as well as those whose prices have increased, underscores the fact that terms such as inflation and deflation refer to average prices across the economy.

Discussion Questions

1. In addition to the consumer goods listed above, can you think of other goods or services whose price has gone down over the past few decades?
2. In 2008, the inflation rate in the United States is approximately 4 percent (CPI). Many producers and consumers worry that this will lead to a wage and price spiral that will be hard to control. Such worries do not exist in command economies. Why?
3. CD players, like other audio consumer goods, are increasingly produced abroad in countries such as Taiwan and South Korea and then imported into the United States. Explain how this can lead to the international transmission of inflation and deflation.

A CONNECTICUT YANKEE IN KING ARTHUR'S COURT

By Mark Twain
New York: Signet Classics, 2004

When Hank Morgan wakes up from a head injury, he finds himself in King Arthur's court some twelve centuries ago. At first the local population distrusts him, but then his education, together with his American values, earns him respect. He manages to escape death and even becomes an important, influential person. People begin to listen to him and follow his suggestions. Hank introduces them to contemporary American technology and helps medieval England achieve a higher standard of living. Problems begin to arise when he tries to introduce a democratic political system where monarchy prevails.

Economic Concepts in *A Connecticut Yankee in King Arthur's Court*

pp. 247–249

Dowley is a blacksmith in medieval England. He and Morgan are having dinner in a local pub. Their conversation is not amicable as both men are touting their own country's superiority. Between bites of overcooked beef, Dowley promotes the benefits of the Kingdom of King Bagdemagus where he resides. Between sips of ruby red wine, Morgan celebrates the superiority of his adopted home, the Kingdom of King Arthur.

In the course of their verbal competition, Dowley invites Morgan to compare typical wages of workers in selected professions. It turns out that the wage of a shepherd in Morgan's country is only 25 milrays while in Dowley's it is double. Morgan states that a mechanic gets paid 50 milrays per day while in Dowley's country he receives 100. With glee, Dowley says he knew it—his country's workers are better paid than their counterparts elsewhere. With more income, it follows that they enjoy a higher standard of living. He has thus proved that the citizens of the Kingdom of King Bagdemagus are the luckiest in the world.

Morgan is not convinced. His knowledge of economics leads him to ask about the cost of living in Dowley's country. Only by comparing those, together with wages, can an assessment be made as to which country's workers are better off.

It turns out that a pound of salt in Dowley's country costs 100 milrays while Morgan pays 40. Dowley pays about 75 milrays for a pound of beef while Morgan pays only 35. For Dowley, a dozen eggs cost 50 milrays while Morgan pays only 20 for the same quantity.

It is Morgan's turn to feel triumphant. He tells his dinner partner, "Your wages are higher than ours only in name." In fact, the wages in Dowley's kingdom have a lower purchasing power than those in Morgan's. They cannot buy the same basket of commodities as the wages in Morgan's land. In comparing wages across borders, the number of coins is irrelevant. What counts instead is how much one can buy with those coins. It turns out that in Morgan's country, people can buy more goods and services with half of a milray than what people in Dowley's country can buy with a full milray. Therefore, Morgan concludes, "Our wages are higher than yours."

Morgan has highlighted the difference between real and nominal wages. Dowley does not understand the terminology or the concepts Morgan is using. Several centuries will pass before people like Dowley come to appreciate the distinction between real and nominal wages.

Discussion Questions

1. If all residents of the Kingdom of King Bagdemagus traveled to the Kingdom of King Arthur to buy the cheaper salt, what would ultimately happen to the price of salt in both kingdoms? If a mechanic from the Kingdom of King Arthur migrated to King Bagdemagus's realm for employment, what would happen to wages in both kingdoms?

2. Having traveled twelve centuries back in time, Morgan can compare modern and medieval prices. He finds that during those centuries, the price of beef has increased in absolute terms. Has it necessarily also gone up in relative terms (that is, relative to other goods and to wages)?

3. Many college students get financial help from a variety of sources in order to pay their educational expenses. What kind of cost-of-living adjustment do those sources typically provide in order to compensate for annual rises in the price of education (including tuition, room, board, books, and fees)?

Chapter 25

Employment

Film: *OVERBOARD*
Fiction: *DEATH OF A SALESMAN*

KEY ECONOMIC CONCEPTS

The *labor force* includes all people over sixteen who are working full time and are not students or institutionalized. It also includes those who are unemployed (the latter is defined as people who are not working but are actively looking for work). The *unemployment rate* refers to the percent of the labor force that is unemployed.

There are several reasons why people are unemployed. *Structural unemployment* refers to unemployment due to the mismatch between the skills of workers and the requirements of employers. When people are laid off due to downturns of the business cycle, it is called *cyclical unemployment*. When people are between jobs or are engaged in a *job search*, it is said that there is *frictional unemployment*.

The labor market consists of *labor demand* and *labor supply* that together determine the wage. When that equilibrium wage is deemed too low, governments set a *minimum wage* below which the price of labor cannot fall. Economists distinguish between *real wages* and *nominal wages* to indicate whether inflation is taken into account.

Employers sometimes discriminate in hiring. Such discrimination occurs on the basis of gender, age, race, and other characteristics and is usually illegal.

Price elasticity of labor supply in the labor market refers to the sensitivity of workers to changes in wages. The more desperate a person is to find work, the higher his or her price elasticity of supply.

OVERBOARD

Rated PG/1987/1hr 53min/Goldie Hawn, Kurt Russell
Directed by Garry Marshall

The spoilt heiress Joanna (Goldie Hawn) leads an empty life. When her yacht is docked on the Pacific coast of Oregon for repairs, she hires a carpenter, Dean (Kurt Russell), to rebuild her closet. She refuses to pay him and even pushes him overboard. But Dean gets his revenge. When later that night Joanna falls from the yacht and loses her memory, Dean recognizes her picture on the news and goes to the hospital to claim her as his wife (her husband didn't bother). Since she has no memory, Dean convinces her that she is the mother of his four misbehaved children. He plans on keeping her until she does enough housework and babysitting to compensate for not paying his wages. She ends up staying much longer since they fall in love.

Economic Concepts in *Overboard*

Scene 3 (1:33–4:00)/ Minutes 9:41–12:08
Scene 8 (0:57–1:59)/ Minutes 23:47–24:48
Scene 12 (0:00–00:22)/ Minutes 35:51–36:13

Joanna is drying her pedicure with a hair dryer while Dean is putting the final touches on the closet he has just built. He beams proudly when he shows Joanna the newly installed mechanism that doubles the shoe space. But Joanna's reaction is not what Dean expected. "You didn't use cedar!" she accuses him, seething. Dean defends himself, claiming he used oak because she never specified which wood she wanted. Joanna's haughty response is, "Everyone in the civilized world knows closets are made out of cedar." With that statement, Joanna implies Dean is uncivilized and by storming out of the room, she underscores her position of power in their work relationship. She has no intention of paying for Dean's labor (two days) plus materials.

Joanna is the employer, and Dean is the employee. They came together in the labor market where he was supplying carpentry labor and she was demanding it. They reached an equilibrium price of $600 including materials. Theirs was a verbal agreement that did not specify the exact nature of his output (namely, a cedar or an oak closet).

This misunderstanding between the unreasonable heiress and the eager carpenter concludes when Joanna pushes Dean overboard and then, to add insult to injury, throws his tool belt and toolbox after him. While watching his hammer and screwdriver sink to the Pacific bottom, Dean is in fact watching the disappearance of the capital inputs that he uses to produce all his carpentry output. Without his tools, Dean's labor productivity is greatly reduced. He had made an investment in those capital inputs and now that they are lost, he has to reinvest in a new set of tools before he can once again supply his labor as a carpenter. But Dean is unemployed and has no savings, so how will he ever come up with money to buy new tools?

The answer to this question comes to him the next day while watching television. The local evening news has a story about a woman retrieved from the ocean who has lost her memory due to a fall. The reporter is inviting people to come forward to identify and reclaim her from the Elk Cove Community Hospital. The face on the screen is unmistakably Joanna's, albeit without makeup, jewelry, and carefully blow-dried hair.

Dean decides to go to the hospital and impersonate her husband. His motivation is rooted in economics (with a sprinkle of revenge). According to Dean's calculations, if he can convince Joanna that she is his wife, she will come live with him and perform the chores of a homemaker. Those chores include taking care of four children, cooking, marketing, cleaning, carpooling, gardening, washing, and ironing. Based on how much Dean pays a housekeeper, Joanna's labor would save him $25 per day. If she performs the chores for twenty-four days, the total value of her work would amount to the $600 she owes him. Dean plans on keeping her an additional six days until she also works off the replacement value of his tools. By Dean's calculations, at the end of the month, Joanna will have paid him in labor what she owed him. He will then return her to the hospital.

If Dean were not unemployed, he might have dismissed his experience on Joanna's boat as an unfortunate episode in his otherwise successful career. He would have amortized the loss of his unpaid labor and capital equipment over many future jobs. But since Dean is unemployed, he is too financially strapped to walk away from $600.

Dean was recently laid off from a full-time job due to a recession that was noted in an earlier scene of *Overboard*. His former employer had to downsize and lay off half of the company workers. Thus Dean became cyclically unemployed. Since then, he has been making ends meet with occasional part-time jobs as a repairman on yachts docked in Elk Cove. However, even those jobs are harder to find now that the prevailing recession has caused decreases in luxury expenditures which means fewer boats to service.

Discussion Questions

1. Dean fires his housekeeper once Joanna moves into his home and takes on household chores. Comment: There is no change in the unemployment rate since one worker is merely replaced by another.

2. California Closets opens a branch in Elk Cove, providing prefabricated shelving units at low prices. What kind of unemployment does Dean now experience?

3. Dean has four children to feed, clothe, and educate. His wife passed away, and he has no family in Oregon to help him out. Imagine that he has a neighbor, Mr. Neighbor, who is also a carpenter. Mr. Neighbor is married to a part-time librarian. While she is at work, Mr. Neighbor's mother-in-law takes care of their kids and cooks dinner. Mrs. Neighbor also tends a vegetable garden that feeds the family. Who has the higher price elasticity of labor supply, Dean or his neighbor?

DEATH OF A SALESMAN

By Arthur Miller
New York: Penguin, 1976
Pulitzer Prize for Drama in 1949

Willy Loman is a traveling salesman who has accomplished little in his life yet continues to have the illusion of greatness. He lives in the past when he still believed life would get better and when he had hope for his two sons. Willy does not recognize just how unhappy his wife is nor what failures his sons are. One day, Willy gets laid off after many years of working in the same company. He then has an argument with his son and, as his world tumbles around him, Willy commits suicide.

Economic Concepts in *Death of a Salesman*

pp. 79–80, 83–84

Willy has summoned the courage to approach his employer Howard and discuss his future at the company. His suit is threadbare and his long body is now stooped over, the weight of life's unhappiness pulling him down. By contrast, Howard is a robust man at the peak of his career. He is busy and has no time for an old has-been like Willy whom he has kept on the payroll only because he was a remnant of his Dad's era—a silly reason rooted in nostalgia. Willy is a traveling salesman who no longer pulls his weight for the company. His labor productivity has steadily declined over the years, and Howard has been looking for an excuse to gently terminate his employment.

Howard gets his excuse the morning Willy tells him he is too tired to travel and would like a desk job in town. Howard explains that there are only half a dozen jobs on the floor. His is mostly a road business that relies on the spread of product information and the sale of merchandise by salesmen who travel from town to town. When Willy realizes Howard will not accommodate his request, he retracts his original complaint and, defeated, says he will go back to traveling. But it is too late. The can of worms has been opened. Howard sees his way out of his predicament. Putting irrational nostalgia aside, he fires Willy.

The dialogue between Howard and Willy illustrates the functioning of the labor market. Howard is still demanding work from traveling salesmen but no longer from Willy. At the same time, Willy continues supplying his labor, even offering to work under increasingly difficult conditions (such as additional travel) in order to remain employed.

Willy is too tired and demoralized to embark on a new job search. Anyway, it is probable he will face discrimination on the basis of age, as employers will not invest in training a worker who is so close to retirement. Willy's unemployment is unlikely to be frictional as he is unlikely to be between jobs. Rather, it is likely he will leave the labor force altogether. If Howard were firing Willy because the company no longer sells merchandise door-to-door with traveling salesmen (but rather conducts sales over the Internet, as is common in the twenty-first century), then Willy's unemployment would be structural.

During Willy's humiliating conversation with Howard, he kept offering to work for lower and lower wages. At first he offered to take a pay cut, down to $65 per week, just to have an office job. After meeting with Howard's intransigence, Willy dropped his asking price to $50. In the end, he even offered to work for $40 just to retain the traveling job he had before he entered Howard's office. Such willingness to accept a lower wage indicates a high price elasticity of supply.

Discussion Questions

1. Can you think of any products that are still sold by traveling salesmen?
2. Reconcile the following two statements. Machines have replaced workers in many industries and so led to higher unemployment (such as Mr. Joad in *The Grapes of Wrath*). Machines, such as computers (that enable e-mail and video conferencing), have increased employment choices for workers as they can now live in one city and work in another.
3. If Howard had agreed to keep Willy on the payroll at $40 per week, what would the hourly wage be (assuming a forty-hour week)? How does that wage compare to the current hourly minimum wage of $7.25? Referring to the previous chapter, explain why the past and present hourly wages are not strictly comparable.

Chapter 26

Personal Income

Film: *TITANIC*
Fiction: *THE GREAT GATSBY*

KEY ECONOMIC CONCEPTS

Economists distinguish between household wealth and income. *Wealth* is the value of all assets (minus liabilities) while *income* refers to money that is received as payment over a period of time.

Individuals pay a *personal income tax* on their income, and the remainder is called *disposable income*. That after-tax income is then either consumed or saved.

TITANIC

Rated PG-13/1997/194 min//Leonardo DiCaprio, Kate Winslet
Directed by James Cameron
Winner of eleven Academy Awards, including Best Picture and Best Director

This movie is about a love story set in 1912 against the background of the sinking ship *Titanic*. Rose (Kate Winslet) is a young woman engaged to Cal Huckley (Billy Zane), a wealthy man she does not love. Together with her mother, they are returning to New York after a prewedding European vacation. However, the wedding will never take place because Rose meets a poor artist on board, Jack Dawson (Leonardo DiCaprio), with whom she falls in love. Even before the ship hits an iceberg, Rose's fiancée and mother learn she has fallen in love with a penniless man and are both angry. When the ship starts sinking, Rose must decide whether to save her life with the first-class passengers or risk drowning with Jack.

Economic Concepts in *Titanic*

Scene 12 (1:47–3:02)/ Minutes 1hr 12:17–1hr 13:32

Rose dresses for dinner in her expansive first-class cabin. Her personal maid fastens the lace corset as Rose's pale face looks forward, an enigmatic look in her eyes. Rose is consumed by feelings of love so beyond anything she has ever felt. By comparison to the indifference (and sometimes disdain) that she feels for her selfish fiancée Cal, Rose's love for Jack has knocked the wind out of her more than any corset ever did. Her thoughts wander to their romantic encounters, those stolen moments enjoyed while avoiding the watchful eye of the conformist society ladies on board the *Titanic*.

Just then Rose's mother walks in, promptly dismissing the maid. She takes over the tying of the corset cords with a ferocity that surprises Rose. With every pull she squeezes Rose's body into a tight-fitting sieve, and with every pull she tries to talk sense into her independent-minded daughter.

The sense she wants to instill has to do with dollars and cents. Money. Marriage. These two words are intricately connected for Rose's mother, who reminds Rose that marriage to Cal is a necessity, not an option. His wealth will bring financial security to both Rose and her mother for as long as they live. It will enable them to maintain the lifestyle to which they are accustomed. Marriage to Cal will earn them social respect and provide them with a secure position in New York's high society. After all, Rose's father lost all the family assets before he died and, while they managed to hide that reality from their friends, their dire financial situation cannot remain secret for very long. The little money they have left is running out.

If Rose fails to marry Cal, all their possessions will soon be sold at auction. At her advanced age, Rose's mother will be forced into the labor market. Sewing is the only skill she has. If she became a seamstress, she would be sewing clothes for the very same ladies she now dines with. The scandal and ensuing embarrassment will be hard to live with as Rose and her mother become the talk of the town and the focus of everyone's pity.

The message sent while weaving the corset cords is that marriage is about wealth, not about love. Therefore, Rose must forget Jack!

For Rose's proud mother with her now watery eyes, Jack is no substitute for Cal. He has no savings, he has no accumulated wealth, and he has no social reputation. Even if he finds employment once he reaches America, Jack would only be earning an income. He would be starting from the bottom of the ladder. By contrast, Cal does not rely on earned income. He does not sell his labor in the labor market but instead lives on interest, and dividends, and coupons paid on investments. The source of his investment money is inheritance. As was the custom at the turn of the twentieth century, wealthy people lived off their investments as working for wages was considered appropriate only for the lower classes.

Given such a worldview, it is understandable that Rose's mother believed Jack's potential for acquiring wealth while struggling as an immigrant artist in New York was low. On that basis she dismissed Jack as an unsuitable contender for her daughter's hand.

By walking away from Cal and linking her life to Jack, Rose knows she will incur an opportunity cost. She is forced to put a price on her love for Jack. Such is the nature of the thoughts filling Rose's mind after the *Titanic* sinks, and she must make on-the-spot decisions about her future.

Discussion Questions

1. If all the protagonists survived and if Jack became employed as a draftsman by a highly regarded architectural firm in New York, Rose's mother would still oppose the marriage between Jack and her daughter. Explain why by highlighting the difference between income and wealth.
2. Would Rose's mother still oppose the marriage to Jack if he robbed a bank and amassed enough wealth to retire at age twenty-five? If so, then what does she value more than wealth?
3. Use key concepts to discuss the following statement: It's not about how much money you earn, it's all about how much money you take home.

THE GREAT GATSBY

By F. Scott Fitzgerald
New York: Simon and Schuster, 1995

It is the roaring twenties. Jay Gatsby lives on Long Island in a huge mansion where he throws exciting parties for New York's high society. He befriends his neighbor, Nick Carraway, who has recently moved from the Midwest to enter the bond business. There is an ulterior motive to that friendship: Nick is the cousin of Daisy, the woman Gatsby loves (even though she is married to Tom). Nick begins to arrange meetings between Gatsby and Daisy, and they soon become lovers. This house of cards falls apart when Tom's mistress is killed in an accident after a confrontation between Daisy, Nick, and Tom. Gatsby is killed soon thereafter, and Nick moves back home, disgusted with the greed and alienation of wealthy New York society.

Economic Concepts in *The Great Gatsby*

pp. 140–141

Tom, Daisy, and Gatsby are all slightly intoxicated, having spent the day lounging around with friends, talking and drinking. They are all jolted out of their complacency when Gatsby announces that he and Daisy love each other and that Daisy plans to leave Tom. Daisy puffs on her cigarette with trembling hands as she openly declares her love for Gatsby.

Tom is incensed, even though he has a mistress (powerful and wealthy men of that time believed they could hold on to both wife and mistress, and they usually did). In a fit of jealousy, he confronts Gatsby with aggressive body language, trying to belittle him in front of Daisy. Tom cannot accuse Gatsby of being a slob, or of being inarticulate, or lazy, or inconsiderate. So he makes the only accusation he can, namely that Gatsby is a crook who has engaged in illegal economic activities. Tom had secretly checked out Gatsby's background and knows he made his fortune in bootlegging.

Bootlegging refers to the sale of alcohol during the Prohibition period (1920–1933) when the federal government made alcohol production, transport, sale, and consumption illegal. As with any illegal activity for which there continues to be demand, entrepreneurial individuals willing to break the law emerge to satisfy the demand. Gatsby is one such entrepreneur. He partneres with the disreputable Meyer Wolfsheim and buys up side street drugstores throughout New York and Chicago. Together with aspirin and face cream, alcohol is sold over the counter.

Bootlegging was a very profitable economic activity. Because it was illegal, suppliers had to take huge risks in producing, transporting, and offering it on the market. Their profits reflected their risks. At the same time, their earnings were not taxed so their total income was equal to their disposable income. Those who managed not to get caught, such as Gatsby, ran a lucrative business and made a bundle of money.

Tom's behind-the-scenes muckraking leads to the public revelation of Gatsby's source of personal income. Although he pretends to the contrary, Gatsby was not born into a wealthy family. Rather, he accumulates wealth over the years through entrepreneurial activities and hard work. After he gets his first break through illegal ventures, Gatsby successfully invests the profits in legal activities. Those activities never entail selling his labor in the market for wages. During the summer described in *The Great Gatsby*, he receives income from his investments.

Discussion Questions

1. The IRS did not tax Gatsby on his bootlegging activities because it did not know about them. Name some contemporary illegal (and profitable) activities that the IRS would benefit from taxing. If these activities are known to the public, why are they not taxed?

2. The government imposes hefty taxes on alcohol sales, and restaurants mark up alcohol prices by some 50 to 200 percent. Still, consumption of alcohol is high. What does that imply about the price elasticity of demand for alcohol? What does it imply about the earnings of alcohol suppliers?

3. Distinguish between wealth and income in your household. Which assets constitute wealth? Which liabilities must you consider in your answer?

Chapter 27

Money

Film: *TRADING PLACES*
Fiction: *ROBINSON CRUSOE*

KEY ECONOMIC CONCEPTS

Money refers to anything that is commonly accepted for payment. Throughout history, a variety of goods have served as money including salt, deerskin, and shells. During earlier times people also used to *barter*, that is, exchange a good or service for another good or service. In modern societies, these forms of payment have largely been replaced by *currency* (including paper money and coins).

In addition to being convenient, currency serves the three basic requirements of money. It is a *unit of account* and so gives users a consistent way of measuring the value of goods. It is an acceptable *medium of exchange* that makes trade among individuals more efficient than barter. Finally, it also serves as a *store of value* that can be used for future purchases.

Real estate, stocks, and valuable paintings are also stores of value. Why then do people demand currency instead of holding all their assets in a house on the shore? People want currency because it is the most liquid way of holding assets. *Liquidity* refers to the ease with which an asset can be transformed into a medium of exchange. A supermarket bill cannot be paid with a painting, but it can be paid with currency.

In addition to currency, *checking accounts* in banks are also very liquid and so are classed together in the narrowest definition of money, namely *M1*.

People hold money (M1) for a variety of reasons. According to the *transactions demand for money*, individuals hold M1 to easily make purchases (or transactions). They also have a *precautionary demand for money* so they hold M1 to guard against unforeseen circumstances.

Increasingly people have come to rely on little plastic cards when making payments. Those come in two varieties: debit and credit cards. *Debit cards* are a convenient form of payment that entails immediate withdrawal from one's bank account. *Credit cards* are fundamentally different as they are short-term bank loans that carry with them cost (a hefty interest rate charge) if payment is not made by the due date.

TRADING PLACES

Rated R/1983/1hr 56min/Eddie Murphy, Dan Aykroyd
Directed by John Landis

The wealthy Duke brothers are greedy and care for no one but themselves. Over the years they have continued to disagree about the role of nature versus nurture: one says the character of a man is based on his nature (characteristics he was born with that are immutable), while the other says it is based on nurture (the environment and circumstances in which he lives). They make a wager that involves transforming a successful executive, Louis Winthorpe III (Dan Aykroyd), into a bum while transforming a bum, Billy Ray Valentine (Eddie Murphy), into an executive. When Valentine finds out about the wager, he seeks out Winthorpe so they can take their revenge.

Economic Concepts in *Trading Places*

Scene 15 (5:40–6:58)/ Minutes 1hr 17:29–1hr 18:44

Valentine now wears three-piece suits and sits in a huge office with a mahogany desk and oriental carpets. He still does not understand the source of the good fortune that placed him in this penthouse office. Just recently he was a petty street bum, pretending to be blind in order to hustle money from unsuspecting pedestrians, while today he is a respected executive with a home just off of Philadelphia's fancy Rittenhouse Square.

In the middle of a workday, Valentine sneaks off to the bathroom for a cigarette. Since his office is in a no-smoking building, he must be careful when satisfying his nicotine urge. Behind a locked stall door, Valentine stands on a toilet seat, balancing precariously so as to exhale straight into a vent. Suddenly he hears the bathroom door swing open, and familiar voices fill the silence. The Duke brothers are just feet away. They are unaware of Valentine and his cigarette as they are thoroughly absorbed in a discussion about a wager. Valentine's ears perk up, and his eyes open wide as he hears their shocking revelation. He has been turned into an executive for a one-dollar bet.

It all comes out. The Duke brothers had a wager that ruined two lives, Winthorpe's and Valentine's. To test their theories about nature vs. nurture, they made Winthorpe destitute and watched him become a liar and a thief in order to survive. In the process, he lost his girlfriend, his job, his home, and his reputation. At the same time, the Duke brothers bestowed wealth and prestige on Valentine and watched him become honest and charitable. But their generosity is reversible. From behind the stall door, Valentine overhears their plan to put him back on the streets now that their wager has ended.

One Duke brother takes a crisp dollar bill from his wallet and hands it to the other. They shake hands with a self-congratulatory air, both proud of their power to mold the world according to their wishes. Two lives are irreparably altered for one dollar. That is how much the Duke brothers value Winthorpe's and Valentine's combined lives. Such a valuation gives a whole new meaning to the question about how much money is a life worth.

In order to make Winthorpe destitute, the powerful and influential Duke brothers cancel his debit and credit cards. In the process, they not only take his identity but they also take away his purchasing power. Moreover, since they changed the locks on Winthorpe's home door, he no longer has access to his belongings. His only asset is the cashmere coat on his back. It is not liquid and cannot easily be sold. Winthorpe has nothing else to use as a medium of exchange and hence cannot make any purchases. He cannot get a haircut, check into a hotel to use the shower, or buy a proper meal.

At the same time, Valentine is given credit cards and abundant cash. For the first time in his life, he has ample purchasing power. For the first time in his life, he eats lobster, wears a Rolex, and has a butler lay out his clothing in the mornings.

Discussion Questions

1. Comment: Instead of asking for cash, beggars would be more successful in satisfying their needs if they offered to barter.
2. After watching *Trading Places*, you probably wonder why Winthorpe did not have a precautionary demand for money before the Duke brothers wager went into effect. Under what conditions would that have helped him avoid destitution?
3. What happens to M1 when Winthorpe's debit cards and bank accounts are turned over to Valentine?

ROBINSON CRUSOE

By Daniel Defoe
New York: Barnes and Noble, 2003

Robinson Crusoe travels across the world in a merchant ship until it is shipwrecked. He manages to swim to the shore of a deserted island where he then spends twenty-eight years with his servant Friday. This book focuses on his survival and the skills he needed to hone in order to stay alive.

Economic Concepts in *Robinson Crusoe*

p. 49

In the first two weeks after the shipwreck, Robinson makes daily trips back and forth from the island to the ship. He goes to the ship empty-handed but returns with as much as one set of hands can carry. Not knowing how much time he has before the weather turns and strong winds sink the wrecked ship, Robinson has prioritized all the items on board according to their expected usefulness in his future life on the island. His muscular body works overtime to dislodge furnishings, cut up wooden slabs, and unscrew metals that can be unscrewed so as to break everything down into manageable size. He then goes back and forth from water to shore, removing first the items he expects to need the most. It is hard physical labor. Robinson's hands are calloused, and his bare back is sunburnt.

On the twelfth day after the shipwreck, Robinson enters the ship's cabin and finds a locker with drawers that had somehow escaped his earlier ransacking. Its contents include two unused razors, one pair of scissors, a dozen knives and forks, and money. The money is cash: thirty-six British pounds as well as some European and Brazilian coins together with some gold and silver coins. In total, this is not an insignificant sum by the standards of the time.

Robinson leaves the cash on board, allowing it to sink during the next storm and be lost forever. This is not an oversight. He is rational when he decides what is worth carrying off the boat. While the cash is obviously a unit of account, it is not a medium of exchange under his present circumstances. On the basis of his initial island exploration, Robinson knows there is no shop where he might use the coins to buy shampoo or sausages. Even if Robinson encounters someone on the island with whom there is scope for trade, it is unlikely that the foreign cash would be an acceptable form of payment. Therefore, the gold, silver, and foreign coins do not give Robinson purchasing power because there is nothing to purchase. In the absence of a transaction demand for that money, he leaves it in the rickety wooden drawer.

However, those coins might have served as a store of value. By saving them for when he returns to civilization, Robinson would have something of value for future use. Also, saving the money for precautionary purposes might enable him to buy his way off the island if an occasion arose.

With the goal of immediate survival in mind, Robinson takes the razors, scissors, and cutlery from the ship. These items will be useful for building shelter, finding and preparing food, and securing safe drinking water.

Discussion Questions

1. Gold coins, such as those Robinson left on the ship, are a popular store of value in many countries. Under what conditions is holding gold more secure than holding dollars?
2. Some tropical island Caribbean countries have developed off-shore financial industries. They appeal to Americans because their laws and tax regulations are more lenient. When Mr. Notax transfers his checking account holdings to one of these island banks, has there been a decrease in the liquidity of his assets? What happens to M1 in the United States?
3. Imagine that one year after Robinson's arrival on the island, a man washes up on shore. He has a pen and a flashlight in his pockets. What are some barter possibilities between the two men?

Chapter 28

Banking

Film: *IT'S A WONDERFUL LIFE*
Fiction: *HARRY POTTER AND THE SORCERER'S STONE*

KEY ECONOMIC CONCEPTS

Banks are institutions that have two primary functions. They accept customers' *deposits* in both savings and checking accounts (typically *savings accounts* pay depositors interest while *checking accounts* give check-writing privileges). Banks also make *loans* for all purposes (including mortgages, student loans, and home improvement loans). In this way, banks bring lenders and borrowers together.

Most banks are *commercial banks* that engage in a wide range of banking activities. There are also *savings and loan associations* that specialize in lending money for mortgages (*mortgages* are loans on real estate). *Credit unions* cater to a group of people who have something in common (such as an employer).

Banks give depositors interest payments on their savings, and they charge borrowers interest on their loans. These two interest rates are different, as borrowers pay more for the privilege of borrowing money than savers get for giving the bank their assets. The difference in interest rates is used to fund bank operations and contributes to *bank profits*.

Bank deposits become part of the bank's *reserves* (reserves are defined as the cash banks have on deposit). A bank cannot lend out all its reserves to borrowers. It keeps a percent of its reserves easily accessible in case depositors want to withdraw their money (this percentage is called the *required reserve ratio*). Only reserves greater than the required reserves can be lent out (these are known as *excess reserves*). By lending out money, which borrowers then deposit in their checking accounts, a cyclical system of *deposit creation* occurs throughout the banking system. Since checking accounts are considered money, namely M1, this process is said to create money.

Usually the amount of money withdrawn is roughly equal to the amount deposited at any given time. However, sometimes many depositors simultaneously want to withdraw money from their accounts. This is called a *bank run*. In earlier times, bank runs often led to a bank's bankruptcy. This no longer happens because the federal government has an insurance scheme that insures each bank deposit up to $100,000 (the Federal Deposit Insurance Corporation, or *FDIC*).

The *Federal Reserve* (also known as the Fed) is the central bank of the United States. It has numerous functions, one of which is to set *monetary policy* that determines the *money supply* in the economy and indirectly the interest rate that the banks will charge. One of the instruments of monetary policy is the required reserve ratio.

IT'S A WONDERFUL LIFE

Rated NR/1946/2hrs 12 min//Jimmy Stewart, Donna Reed
Directed by Frank Capra

George Bailey (Jimmy Stewart) has spent his life helping others in the small town where he grew up. Even though he has big dreams, after his father dies he takes over the family savings bank, the Bailey Building and Home Society. Many of the townsfolk get their mortgages from George, and at very good terms with more flexibility. For George, the bank is more than a business, it is a way of helping people. That is in contrast to his competitor Mr. Potter, who is always on the lookout for ways to push George into bankruptcy. But no matter how much he tries, he does not succeed because the town's grateful population ultimately comes out in force to help George.

Economic Concepts in *It's a Wonderful Life*

Scene 12 (3:04–7:18)/ Minutes 53:17–57:30

George and Mary are in a taxi, en route to the train station. They are about to embark on a greatly anticipated trip abroad to celebrate their honeymoon in romantic Paris. Driving down the town's main street, they notice a crowd of people at the entrance of George's bank. Umbrellas collide as people shuffle nervously against each other. Others run down the street towards the crowd, undeterred by the rain. Although Mary wants to ignore the commotion and proceed with their travel plans, George cannot resist checking it out. He emerges from the taxi and then, with his determined quick stride, makes his way to the bank. It doesn't take long for him to realize what is happening. It is a run on the bank.

George gently elbows his way through the congregation of bank depositors, many of whom he salutes by name. After he unlocks the bank's front gate, they spill inside, all holding their savings books in hand (in that time, account activity was recorded in booklets that savers brought to the bank for withdrawals). A relative who helps George run the bank, Uncle Billy, is already inside and promptly explains what led to this crisis.

Apparently an unnamed bank, that had earlier lent money to Bailey Building and Home Society, called in their loan before the due date. Under pressure, Uncle Billy had to turn over all the cash there was on the bank premises, and still the loan was not repaid in full. As a result, there was zero cash in Bailey's drawers to satisfy the random depositors who came to make withdrawals. When Uncle Billy could not honor their requests, they panicked and spread the word. News travel fast in small towns, and immediately other depositors came forth demanding their money as well.

As George tries to resolve the problem and still salvage his honeymoon, the phone rings. It is Mr. Potter, the town's richest man. He has a reputation for buying up everything that is for sale and making offers on what is not. He has been trying to buy George's bank for a long time and now sees an opportunity to succeed. Feigning concern, Potter asks George, "Is there anything I can do? There is a rumor that you have closed your door." With cunning, Potter proposes the following: If George sends his customers over to him, they will receive fifty cents for each dollar they had deposited with George. In the meantime, Potter will guarantee to give the unnamed bank sufficient money to pay George's loans. By implication, in return for these favors, George needs to close his bank doors and declare bankruptcy. Such action allows Potter to buy up Bailey Home Society and become the sole moneylender in town.

Although George is between a rock and a hard place, he refuses to give in to Potter. Instead, he hangs up the phone and heads to the waiting room to reason with his agitated depositors. They need a lesson in economics.

George personalizes the concept of money creation by explaining how each one of them is part of the bank borrowing and lending cycle. He points to one panicked depositor and tells him how his deposit is tied up in Joe's house and then points to Joe, standing nearby. "Your deposit is in the Kennedy house," he says, pointing again, "and her deposits are in

Mrs. Maplin's house." If they each try to withdraw their deposits, they are in effect calling in the loans held by their friends and neighbors. When aggregated across all depositors, such behavior inevitably results in foreclosures and evictions. "Is that what you want?" George asks a few random depositors.

Alas, such reasoning is beyond the comprehension of many in the room. Some clutch their savings booklets to their chests, as though protecting them from oncoming disaster. Others wave their booklets with extended arms, not seeing past their immediate desire to hold their cash in their hands. George stands perplexed and deflated, not knowing what to do next.

At that moment, his new bride Mary comes to the rescue. She had made her way into the bank lobby and stood inconspicuously against a wall, the raindrops still wet on her coat. And now she steps forward, waving a stack of cash. It is the money allocated for their Paris honeymoon. Mary selflessly offers it to George to distribute among his depositors.

Mary's contribution is insufficient to satisfy all the depositors' demands, so another economics lesson is in order. George states that, according to the papers they all signed when their savings accounts were first opened, each depositor must give the bank a sixty-day notice before withdrawing their money. This stipulation distinguishes a savings account (that pays interest) from a checking account (that does not pay interest). It exists at the Bailey Building and Home Society, a savings and loan association, as well as at the unnamed commercial bank that Bailey owes money to.

It's a Wonderful Life depicts the banking industry before the creation of the Federal Reserve. Since then, there are clear stipulations as to the proportion of deposits that must be kept as required reserves and therefore how much is left for lending in the form of excess reserves. These requirements, set forth by the Federal Reserve, serve to prevent runs on banks such as the one depicted on film.

Since the FDIC had not yet been created, George's depositors do not have federal insurance. For that reason some are willing to take Potter's offer of fifty cents to the dollar, which they correctly deem is better than losing all their money. If the FDIC had existed, Mary would not have to give up her honeymoon in order to appease George's panicked depositors.

Discussion Questions

1. Mary's purse contained $2,000 in cash to pay for honeymoon expenses. Explain why this is improbable in contemporary society, and what other payment options do modern honeymooners have?
2. If you or your family owns a home, where did you get your mortgage? If it was from a building and loan association, why did you choose

that over a commercial bank? Explain why building and loan associations continue to exist when commercial banks also provide mortgages?

3. In the absence of federal regulations pertaining to bank required reserves, what might George have done differently to forestall a run on his bank?

HARRY POTTER AND THE SORCERER'S STONE

By J. K. Rowling
New York: Scholastic, 1999

Harry Potter was a baby when his parents died in a car accident. He was raised by his relatives, the Dursleys, with whom he spent ten unhappy years. His cousin Dudley was a bully who did mischievous things and blamed them on Harry. While growing up, Harry was becoming increasingly aware that he was different from other people and that he had unique powers. Around his tenth birthday, he gets a letter saying he has been accepted to the Hogwarts School of Witchcraft and Wizardry. The Dursleys don't want to let Harry go, but they cannot resist the giant Hagrid who shows up at their house and takes Harry away for his many adventures at school.

Economic Concepts in *Harry Potter and the Sorcerer's Stone*

pp. 72–75

Hagrid takes Harry to London to shop for uniforms, books, and magician's tools that he will need in order to enroll at the Hogwarts School of Witchcraft and Wizardry. However, before they can buy anything, Hagrid and Harry stop off at a bank to withdraw some of Harry's inheritance. After all, Hagrid tells the young and impressionable Harry, you cannot make purchases without money.

The bank is housed in a tall white building that towers over the adjoining little shops. It has huge bronze doors that are manned by a goblin in a scarlet and gold uniform. Walking past the guard to whom Hagrid nods in salute, Harry finds himself in a huge hall made of marble floors, marble ceilings, and marble walls. The scene is not significantly different from what one might find in any contemporary bank except that the staff consists entirely of goblins. They perform banking activities typical of contemporary banks. Goblins greet customers while seated behind a counter (they have to sit on high stools given their size). They record evidence of bank transactions (although they use ledgers instead of computers). They count money (actually, they weigh coins on brass scales rather than put bills through counting machines). And they escort customers back and forth between their safe deposit boxes.

A goblin named Griphook is assigned to take Harry and Hagrid to the safe that contains Harry's inheritance. Griphook leads them down a steeply inclined passageway lit by torches where they board a cart that hurtles along floor tracks. When they arrive to the appropriate door, Griphook turns the key, green smoke seeps out, and the door opens. There are mounds of gold coins, columns of silver, and heaps of bronze Knuts (magic currency) on the floor of a windowless room. Harry's eyes become round behind his oversized glasses. This is all his!

Harry's parents had left their wealth to their son in a safe deposit box (although, given its magnitude, it required a room rather than a box). By placing it there for safekeeping, they withdrew the money from circulation and thus decreased England's money supply. They did not deposit their money in a commercial bank where it would have become a part of the bank reserves. Their money did not count towards the bank's required reserves or its excess reserves. Their numerous coins did not contribute to money creation within the British banking system.

If Harry's parents had deposited their money in a mainstream commercial bank in London, Harry would have earned interest on his deposits. Ten years after the deposit was made, there would have been a hefty increase in the quantity of gold, silver, and Knuts in Harry's inheritance.

It is likely that Harry's parents did contribute to the bank's profits by paying a fee for the safekeeping of their inheritance. Part of that fee probably paid for polishing the marble floors.

Discussion Questions

1. What is the opportunity cost of placing Harry's inheritance in the magician's bank? Who incurs this cost, Harry or his parents?
2. Had there been a run on the magician's bank, would Harry's inheritance have been affected? Explain.
3. If there were a similar magician's bank in the United States, what rules would it have had to follow in order to become part of the Federal Reserve system?

Chapter 29

Government Revenue and Expenditure

Film: *DAVE*
Fiction: *CANDIDE*

KEY ECONOMIC CONCEPTS

The federal government intervenes in the economy in order to help society achieve the goals of economic growth, price stability, and full employment. With one or more of those goals in mind, the government formulates programs and policies. Spending on these is called *government expenditure* and is financed by *government revenue*, most of which comes from taxes. The use of government expenditure and/or *taxation* to achieve economic goals is called *fiscal policy*.

When the government seeks to expand economic activity in order to achieve its goals, then *expansionary fiscal policy* is pursued (this is achieved by increasing spending and/or lowering taxes). Alternatively when its goals call for decreased economic activity, then *contractionary fiscal policy* is introduced (namely, the decrease in spending and/or the increase in taxes).

When government expenditure is equal to government revenue then there is a *balanced budget*. More often than not, expenditures exceed revenues, and the government has a *budget deficit*. In that case, the expenditure is financed with borrowing. The *national debt* is the accumulation of these deficits. Alternatively, when government expenditure is less than revenue then there is a *budget surplus*.

DAVE

Rated PG-13/1993/105 minutes/Kevin Kline, Sigourney Weaver
Directed by Ivan Reitman

Dave Kovic (Kevin Kline) looks just like the mean and unscrupulous president, Bill Mitchell. Dave is a nice guy who runs an employment agency. One day the president has a stroke, and his chief of staff Bob Alexander (Frank Langella) comes up with a plan. He recruits Dave, who has acting experience, to be a stand-in until the president recovers. In the meantime, the chief of staff intends to run the country by controlling Dave, his puppet proxy. But things don't go according to his plan. While performing presidential functions in the White House, Dave develops a crush on the First Lady (Sigourney Weaver). He takes the opportunity to make economic and political policy changes that conform to his (and her) values. The First Lady is drawn to Dave while the chief of staff is furious. In the end, Dave identifies an ingenious exit strategy that hurts only the bad guys.

Economic Concepts in *Dave*

Scene 15 (00:40–4:16)/ Minutes 55:37–59:13

The First Lady is an impassioned supporter of homeless shelters while the president wants to veto the Simpson Gardner works bill that funds them. His veto would close down numerous shelters across the country. While there is sufficient money in the budget, the president has other priorities and chooses to spend government revenue on programs that do not benefit the homeless.

Then the president has a stroke, and Dave takes his place in the Oval Office. At first Dave treads carefully in his new acting role, allowing his strings to be pulled by chief of staff Alexander. But with time he becomes emboldened, realizing that he has a unique opportunity to change policy and make a difference. After Alexander fakes the presidential veto of the works bill, Dave decides to use his position as "president" to overturn the veto and save the shelters. Having recently visited one with the First Lady, he was genuinely moved by the plight of the homeless children.

Dave invites his friend Murray, an accountant, to review the federal budget and come up with a way to save the shelters. Over bratwurst with mustard, Dave and Murray pour over the budget statistics, drowning in numbers late into the night. And then, bingo, they figure it out. Dave decides to present his new plan at a scheduled Cabinet meeting the next morning. He even invites the press to watch.

To the dismay of the chief of staff, Dave walks into the meeting seemingly more confident and presidential than usual. He surprises all those present by adding a discussion of the federal budget to the agenda. Without beating about the bush, Dave states his intention to come up with $650 million to fund the homeless shelters. It can be done, he states, by making some tough choices about how the government spends money.

He first hones in on expenditures of the Defense Department, which, Dave informs the audience, has been paying seventeen defense contractors even though they have been delinquent on their contracts. With genuine innocence, Dave suggests that the government hold back the cash until the contractors perform the work. That cash could be put into a simple savings account and in only one year, the interest would amount to $23 million. Dave writes these numbers on a pad of paper and does simple arithmetic with a pencil. Meanwhile all eyes in the room bounce back and forth between him and the now undeniably uncomfortable defense secretary. Lined up against the walls of the room, reporters are frantically taking notes. Cameras are flashing.

Next, Dave explains that the Commerce Department is running a $47 million ad campaign to boost U.S. confidence in domestic automobile purchases. With slightly raised eyebrows, Dave turns to the commerce secretary and says, "I don't want to tell some poor eight-year-old kid that he'll be out on the street so that we can feel better about cars we've already purchased. Do you?" More camera flashes, and the secretary has no alternative but to say that no, he doesn't.

After Dave fills a page with calculations, he victoriously announces that he has come up with $656 million. The homeless shelter is saved, and the applause is thunderous (and the chief of staff is fuming as his fiscal policy plans have been derailed).

Funding the homeless shelter did not require raising taxes. It did not require borrowing money or deficit spending. There are no additions to the national debt. Instead, through simple money management together with some tough choices, sufficient money was made available for the shelters. The composition of federal expenditures was changed. Since there has been no change in the quantity of expenditure, funding the shelters did not constitute new expansionary fiscal policy.

Dave's single-minded focus made the formulation of fiscal policy seem simple. Outside Hollywood, it is not so easy. Decision-makers, faced with insufficient resources, must balance numerous competing goals and make hard choices that involve trade-offs and opportunity costs. All that happens against a background of highly motivated lobbyists that apply intense pressure in support of their interest groups.

Discussion Questions

1. Comment: The federal government is just like me. It has many goals and has to juggle many commitments. The only difference is that when I

want to spend more money than I have, I use a MasterCard, whereas Washington doesn't have one.

2. The reporters at the Cabinet meeting are wildly enthusiastic about Dave's proposal to fund the homeless shelter. Imagine if one of them asked Dave how his proposal helps the country achieve the goals of economic growth and full employment. How might Dave have answered?

3. Most politicians know that in order to fund projects such as homeless shelters (or Medicare or highway repairs), the government must raise money through taxation. Yet, when they campaign for election, politicians typically tout their planned expenditures but rarely mention the taxes that are needed to fund them. Why do you think politicians are reluctant to tell the electorate they might raise taxes?

CANDIDE

By Voltaire
New York: Bantam Classic, 1981

This book is about the unbelievable mishaps of Candide, starting from his youth in a German baron's castle to his old age in rural France. He is the quintessential optimist, a man for whom the glass is always full, even when there is not a drop of water inside. Candide travels across the world, not out of choice but rather as a result of a series of unfortunate events that happen to him, his tutor Pangloss, and his childhood love, Cunégonde (these include war, famine, murder, slavery, the Inquisition, disease, rape, and cannibalism, among others). Candide retains his optimism throughout, and in the end they all settle down to live a calm life on a little farm.

Economic Concepts in *Candide*

p. 65

At one point in his long string of mishaps, Candide finds himself roaming through South America with his Peruvian valet, Cacambo. They come across a deserted boat. Having no other options and nothing left to lose, they board the boat and allow themselves to drift with the current. After a few days journey, the river narrows and flows into a tunnel under high mountains with unscalable precipices. When Candide and Cacambo finally emerge from the darkness, they find themselves in a land different from anything they had ever seen. The roads are literally paved with stones made of gold and silver. Richly dressed people ride in ornate carriages adorned with precious stones. Children dressed in gold brocade clothing play ball with huge emeralds and rubies. The wealthy have homes with gold doors (while those of their poor neighbors are made of silver). Drinking fountains dispense liquors and immaculately maintained parks are dotted with oversized fruits and flowers. It is truly a land of plenty (and is appropriately called Eldorado—The Golden, in Spanish).

The two astonished men wander about, not resisting the temptation to fill their pockets with some gold nuggets lying around by the roadside. They are hungry and tired by the time they come upon a castle more elaborate than those of Europe. Learning that it is an inn, they step inside and are immediately welcomed as important guests. Waiters dressed in gold cloth serve them huge platters of flavorful food. At no time does Candide wonder how he will pay for this feast—he knows that his pockets are now full of gold.

Between mouthfuls, Candide and Cacambo take time to look around, soaking up their surroundings. The inn is full of men who, it turns out, are traveling merchants engaged in trade across the land. Candide and Cacambo strike up a conversation, curious about this incredible country and wanting to learn more about it. They are told that in Eldorado people often live to 172. Everyone is happy because everyone has everything they want. There are no shortages of anything. As a result, there is no crime and therefore no courts of law and no prisons. Candide cannot believe his ears as he is comparing this socioeconomic miracle to the disharmony, poverty, inequality, and scarcity he left back home in medieval Europe.

Having eaten and drunk to their heart's content, Candide reaches into his pocket to retrieve two big pieces of gold. He places them on the table in payment for their meal, figuring he is being generous as that amount of gold could buy hundreds of meals in his home country. Yet his gesture is met with ridicule by the inn's host and hostess. Laughing at the sight of his payment, they ask in amazement, "You're paying us with stones? Clearly you are not from our country."

Candide learns that gold is so abundant in Eldorado that its value is too low for it to serve as payment. But more importantly, Candide learns that there is no charge for their meal since the government will pick up their tab. In fact, the government of Eldorado runs all the country's inns for the convenience of its travelers and merchants. Such government expenditure subsidizes merchants and motivates them to engage in commerce. By trading, these merchants stimulate the economy. The government subsidies have additional consequences, including an expansionary effect on supporting industries such as the accommodation and food and beverage industries. By way of the multiplier process, government expenditure results in increased employment and production, two goals that are often at the root of fiscal policy.

Unanswered is the question of where Eldorado's government gets the revenue to fund its expenditures. Is there a tax system? Does the government print money or an equivalent of money? Is there an abundant budget surplus that it draws on? Does it borrow from a source beyond the mountains, or does it issue treasury bonds? The only hint that readers of *Candide* are given is that there is no scarcity in Eldorado. In the absence of scarcity, choices, trade-offs, and opportunity costs are fundamentally altered. It is likely that Eldorado's public sector resources are so large that fewer choices need to be made since more expenditures can be funded (to twenty-first-century readers, such lack of scarcity brings to mind a contemporary example of seemingly unlimited resources, namely the Dubai Emirate).

Clearly public expenditure in Eldorado is not funded by the abundant gold and precious stones scattered throughout the land, as they are not valuable enough. That is why the government budget is not affected when Candide ultimately leaves the country with his pockets full of gold and diamonds (trying to get himself to Europe to live out his life as a rich man).

Eldorado is a closed economy. Its leaders have decided not to have contact with outsiders because they fear more powerful countries will invade if they learn about its riches. This policy implies that the population can satisfy its needs without international trade; that is, with no exports of its products and no imports from outside markets. The geography of Eldorado lends itself to such autarky as the high mountain peaks and treacherous paths help ensure no outsider trespasses (it is by pure accident that Candide found his way there).

Discussion Questions

1. Eldorado has a closed economy. What would have to be true in the twenty-first century for a country to survive as a closed economy? How does the Internet and global cell phone service affect efforts to keep an economy closed?

2. When subsidizing merchants, the government of Eldorado is also indirectly helping other businesses by creating a demand for their output. For example, merchant activity results in demand for carriage services (transportation) and leather goods (luggage). How might the government use fiscal policy to tap those industries so as to recoup some of its expenditure on merchant subsidies?

3. Imagine: Candide reaches France with his pockets full of gold and precious stones. At the border, he is asked to declare everything he acquired abroad. The customs authorities assess the value of his possessions and order him to pay a tax (also known as an import tax or tariff). Discuss the effect of that tax on France's government revenues, expenditures, and annual budget.

Chapter 30

Government Intervention

Film: *CRASH*
Fiction: *THE JUNGLE*

KEY ECONOMIC CONCEPTS

In order to achieve social and economic goals, the government intervenes in the economy in a variety of ways. It uses revenue from taxation in order to redistribute income throughout society. *Redistribution* takes the form of taxing those with higher incomes and making transfer payments to those with lower incomes. *Transfer payments* are payments made by the federal government to households that provide no goods or services in return (transfer payments include social security, welfare, and unemployment benefits). Such redistribution is deemed to be in the best *social interest*.

Another form of government intervention entails *regulation* of economic activity. This happens in both the factor and product markets. In the factor market, government sets the *minimum wage* of workers (this is a *price floor* and wages cannot by law fall below it). Government also sets standards for health and safety in the workplace, as well as requiring that some benefits be mandatory.

With respect to the product market, government intervention occurs with the purpose of protecting consumers from selected economic activities. In addition to curtailing the market power of monopolies, government regulates food and drug safety as well as environmental pollution. To different extents and at different times, government has regulated specific industries such as airlines, trucking, oil, gas, electricity, cable, and telephone. Such regulation, while beneficial to many consumers, also has the effect of increasing the cost of production and thereby reducing supply.

CRASH

Rated R/2005/1 hr 53 min/Sandra Bullock, Don Cheadle, Matt Dillon
Directed by Paul Haggis
Winner of three Academy Awards, including Best Picture

In this film, the lives of seemingly unrelated people of Los Angeles are shown during a thirty-six hour period. The people are very diverse: they are rich and poor, working and unemployed, white, black, Asian, and Hispanic. Their paths cross in intricate ways, illustrating both their good and their bad sides. Indeed, the cop, the district attorney, the shop owner, and, the movie mogul all have human qualities while at the same time they are full of prejudices and hatred.

Economic Concepts in *Crash*

Scene 10 (1:33–4:09)/ Minutes 46:24–49:01; (NOTE: this scene contains vulgar language.)

Ryan, an L.A. cop, is unsatisfied, underpaid, and stressed out. He lives with his ailing father, and together they do not have sufficient combined income to hire a nurse's aide. Ryan assists his father with all his personal needs and has come to believe the illness is more serious than what has been diagnosed by an overworked HMO doctor. However, his inadequate health insurance plan does not allow him to go out of the plan network for a second medical opinion without special dispensation. Frustrated by the system and concerned by his father's rapidly deteriorating condition, Ryan takes time from work and sets out to personally plead for such dispensation with the administrator of his father's health insurance.

Unfortunately for him, the administrator turns out to be the same Ms. Shaniqua Johnson who was on the other end of the phone when Ryan lost his temper during an earlier conversation. He had insulted her with disparaging racist comments that she has not forgotten. Now she is sitting behind a desk, looking professional and speaking eloquently, while Ryan's arms are folded on his chest in a passive aggressive stance. In a scene that clearly highlights her position of power, Ms. Johnson denies Ryan's request.

This provokes a verbalization of the disgust Ryan feels towards federal regulation and involvement in the economy. At the root of his emotion lies his father's lifelong experience. Starting his work life as a janitor decades ago, Ryan Sr. saved enough money to start his own company. For thirty years he worked side-by-side with twenty-three employees, all minorities. Even though he paid wages that were higher than those of his competitors, he did not waver from his belief that such wages were fair (by implication, he paid more than the minimum wage stipulated by the government when it intervenes in the labor market). Then one day, the government introduced policies of affirmative action in an effort to discriminate in favor of minorities who are often discriminated against. These policies applied to various sectors of the economy, including business. In conformance with the law, the City Council decides to give minority-owned businesses preference in all their contracts. As a result, Ryan Sr. can no longer compete and goes out of business, losing his home in the process.

Ryan blames government regulation for ruining his father's life, telling Ms. Johnson, "He lost everything so that people like you could benefit."

Adding insult to injury, Ryan accuses an incredulous Ms. Johnson of getting her current job because of similar regulation, at the expense of five or six better qualified white men.

Ryan's rant, cut off by a security guard who comes to escort him out of the building, raises important questions about government policies that are made in the social interest. What serves the best interest of some individuals can simultaneously hurt others, thus poignantly raising the question of what exactly is the social interest.

Discussion Questions

1. Apply the concept of social interest to mandated minority advantage in college admissions.
2. Comment: Progressive taxes redistribute income among members of society. In that way, everyone gets what he or she deserves.
3. When Ryan Sr. owned his company, he paid all twenty-three workers above minimum wage. What would have happened to his company's costs, output, and employment if new government regulation stipulated that each worker be given employer-sponsored health insurance?

THE JUNGLE

By Upton Sinclair
New York: Barnes and Noble Classics, 2005

Like many immigrants during his time, Jurgis Rudkus comes to America to pursue the American dream. He starts off working in Chicago's meatpacking industry where conditions are revolting. He and his family join other Lithuanian immigrants in a neighborhood where they are tricked into buying a house that is beyond their means. Every member of the Rudkus household, both the oldest and the youngest, must work to earn an income as every penny is needed for survival. Things go from bad to worse when a boy is poisoned and a grandfather has an injury and Jurgis's wife is raped at work. When Jurgis seeks revenge, he is sent to jail and his family gets evicted from their home for lack of payment. This book is a classic about the immigrant experience and the injustices experienced in the chase for the American dream.

Economic Concepts in *The Jungle*

p. 107

Jurgis spoke very little English when he signed the deed to his house. He had no friends or family who spoke English well enough to understand the fine print. And anyway, there were unforeseen contingencies associated with home ownership that were not in the contract but still proved to be very real and expensive. For example, no one told him he was required to pay for home insurance, nor that water pipes can freeze, burst, and cause a flood.

After yet one more mishap with his house, Jurgis begins to think he has been conned into buying and overpaying for the property. He decides to confront the real estate agent, to demand he be told exactly and truthfully all the expenses for which he is responsible. Stewing, Jurgis walks all the way downtown in the frigid air of an Illinois winter, his breath a white cloud lingering around his face.

But the agent is no longer interested in spending time with this illiterate immigrant from some old country. The deed has already been signed, and the agent has already collected his cut. Every additional minute spent with Jurgis represents an opportunity cost. Nevertheless, the agent decides to talk to Jurgis so as to get rid of him once and for all. Now there is no more reason to sugarcoat the real estate deal and to deceitfully skip over the details that Jurgis wouldn't see for himself. And so the agent tells Jurgis, in a tone that is both sarcastic and disdainful, all the payments he has to look forward to as a homeowner in America.

In addition to monthly mortgage installments and interest payments, Jurgis also has to pay for home insurance every year. That insurance is not comprehensive and has large deductibles.

"And then there are the taxes," the agent says, watching sadistically the effect of his words. Jurgis learns that he has to pay $10 per year for the homeowners tax and another $6 for the water tax. The agent blows cigarette smoke in Jurgis's face before adding, "That is all, unless the city decides to put in a sewer or to lay a sidewalk." The sewer costs $22, and the sidewalk's price is $15 if made of wood, $25 if cement.

Jurgis is told that he has no choice. By law, taxes have to be paid.

The agent lays out the government regulations pertaining to the financial responsibility of the neighborhood's residents. The government taxes all people so as to accumulate revenue with which to make expenditures that are believed to be in the best interests of society (such as putting in a sewer system that improves public health or building a sidewalk that prevents accidents). It is through the taxation system that the cost of a government project is shared by those who will benefit from it. Choices about projects, such as sidewalks and sewage systems, are made by elected officials who represent the residents. The agent is clear about this: it is the city officials that decide if and when to put in a sewer. They decide if the sidewalk will be made of wood or cement.

During his conversation with the agent, Jurgis decides that he will save on the water tax by turning off the hydrant. He fails to distinguish between water usage and the water tax. His water bill reflects how much water his household consumes while the water tax is assessed by household, irrespective of use. Turning off the hydrant will not save him the water tax payment. Instead, it might get him in trouble with the city for tinkering with government property.

Discussion Questions

1. Why do public schools in wealthy neighborhoods have more resources (such as computers and sports equipment) than public schools in poor neighborhoods?

2. Sweden has one of the highest income tax rates in the world, and yet taxation is rarely at the heart of political debate at election time as it is in the United States. What does this imply about the way voters in both countries perceive their tax dollars are being spent?

3. The publication of *The Jungle* led to the creation of the Food and Drug Administration in 1906. It also led to legislation pertaining to food safety and meat inspection. A century has passed, and food safety is still an issue (witness e-coli, mad cow disease, salmonella, etc). Does this imply we need more regulation? Different regulation? No regulation?

Chapter 31

Inequality and Poverty

Film: *THE NOTEBOOK*
Fiction: *HARD TIMES*

KEY ECONOMIC CONCEPTS

While it is obvious that there are many poor people in the United States, the extent of *poverty* is measured by using the federal government's *poverty line*. This poverty line refers to the minimum amount of income considered sufficient for an adequate standard of living (in 2008, it was $21,200 for a family of four). All those whose incomes fall below the poverty line are said to be poor.

The federal government's program of transfer payments seeks to enable those below the poverty line to improve their *standard of living*.

In addition to measuring absolute poverty, economists also seek to understand relative poverty—in other words, how poor are people relative to others. Clearly not all individuals in society have the same income but rather, *income inequality* is the norm. In order to understand just how unequal the distribution of income is, economists look at the quintile distribution. Household incomes are divided into five categories, and the total income in each group is compared. In a perfectly equal society, the top fifth of the population receives one-fifth of the total income, as does the bottom fifth. In reality, the top fifth receives much more.

Many factors are responsible for fostering poverty and inequality in society. These include factors inherent in individuals (such as education, inherited wealth, and innate abilities) as well as those that are a product of social circumstances (including unemployment and discrimination).

While many people say inequality is not fair, economists shy away from talking about *fairness.* It is considered a normative concept while economics deals with positive concepts (*positive analysis* refers to the way things are while *normative analysis* refers to the way things should be). However, to the extent that governments introduce redistributive policies as well as laws against discrimination (such as *affirmative action* that includes policies increasing representation of minorities), it might be said that those are aimed at increasing fairness in society (note: affirmative action was introduced in chapter 30 as an example of government intervention in the economy).

THE NOTEBOOK

Rated PG-13/2004/2 hr 4 min/Ryan Gosling, Rachel McAdams
Directed by Nick Cassavetes

Allie (Rachel McAdams) and her wealthy Charleston family have a vacation home in a small southern town. In the summer of her seventeenth year, Allie meets a local boy, Noah (Ryan Gosling). They begin dating and soon fall madly in love. However, Allie's parents don't understand their relationship as Noah is a poor lumberjack with no prospects while Allie is headed for college in the fall. They cut their summer vacation short and take Allie away from Noah. A few years later, the two meet again and their passion is rekindled. Allie has to choose between a rural life with Noah and a city life with a wealthy Southerner. The story of Noah and Allie's love is written in a notebook that an elderly man (James Gardner) regularly reads to his elderly companion (Gena Rowlands) in their old age home.

Economic Concepts in *The Notebook*

Scene 5 (7:00–8:38)/Minutes (26:11–27:50)
Scene 7 (1:30–4:30)/ Minutes (38:18–41:18)

Allie's parents invite Noah to join them for a luncheon at their summer home. It is to be their first meeting, and Noah is nervously counting the days until Sunday. Although he knows Allie is rich, he is not prepared for what he sees.

Behind an imposing wrought iron gate lies an equally imposing mansion surrounded by acres of land. At the far side of the main building, overlooking a lake, a long table is set with flowing white linen. Porcelain plates, crystal glasses, and silver cutlery all sparkle in the bright daylight.

A white canvas tent covers the table area to protect the lily-white complexions of the guests from the ravages of the summer sun. Multiple servers hover around the party, ensuring that no glass is ever empty for too long. It is obvious that all the guests belong to wealthy Southern society accustomed to outings such as this one. All guests except for one: Noah.

By contrast to his girlfriend's luxurious abode, Noah shares a modest two-room home with his father. They take turns cooking as they take turns driving the family truck. Noah and his father are by no means the poorest people in rural South Carolina, and it is doubtful that they fall below the poverty line. There are many others in the vicinity that have no steady jobs, live ten to a shack, and subsist on food from a garden patch outside their front door. However, by comparison to Allie's family, Noah and his dad are poor and hardly distinguishable from their less fortunate neighbors.

In a mere few scenes of *The Notebook*, the distinction between absolute and relative poverty is illustrated. In the course of lunch, one of the guests turns to Noah and inquires what he does for a living. Expecting to hear about a family business or a Harvard education, the guests are visibly rattled when Noah responds that he is a lumberjack. Innocently, he goes on to describe what exactly he does at the local lumberyard. Another incredulous guest then asks how much he gets paid, obviously wondering how Noah can afford to take Allie on a date. When Noah responds that his wage is forty cents per hour, silence descends upon the table. Heads turn towards Allie's parents to gauge their reaction to this shocking revelation. After all, the guests at the table own lumberyards, they don't work in them. Allie's mother's lips form into a thin line and her eyes narrow, and it is clear what she is thinking: this boy does not belong with us.

The reality that Noah and Allie belong to different income groups is highlighted at this luncheon. Allie is undoubtedly in the uppermost quintile of American society while Noah is probably in the bottom fourth.

While quintiles are determined on the basis of wealth or income, the division of society that they describe applies also to opportunity. Without a doubt, those in the top quintile have greater life opportunities than those in the bottom quintile. For example, Allie is headed to college to obtain a higher education while there is no education in Noah's future. After college, Allie will have a broad range of employment options (although she is unlikely to take any of them, given the social norms of her time for women of her social background). Not having obtained a college degree, Noah's employment prospects will be no greater than they were when he first started working at the lumberyard. Allie will visit Europe, sail a boat, learn a foreign language, and play the piano. Noah is unlikely to do any of those.

Several weeks after that sobering luncheon, Allie's parents take steps to ensure the line between income groups does not get crossed. It happens when Allie and Noah stay out late one night. Upon their return there are tears and raised voices as social prejudices emerge in full force. Allie's mother accuses Noah of being "trash, trash, trash." More words about class boundaries and income differences and college education and future opportunities fill the heavy air of that night. Noah is depicted as a threat to the existing social order. The very next day, Allie's parents board up the house for the summer and move the family back to Charleston.

Discussion Questions

1. Allie is headed for Sarah Lawrence College in the fall while Noah has no higher education opportunities. How have the education (and therefore earning) possibilities for rural southern teenagers changed since before World War II, especially for those as motivated and bright as Noah?
2. Although Noah and his dad are poor, they are very close and often sit together on their porch, reading and chatting. Allie's dad is rich, but he never seems to have time for her. Comment: Wealth, quality of life, and standard of living are unrelated.
3. Comment: Noah's dad sits around on his porch because his opportunity cost of time is low. He would be a better father if he found a decent job and saved money for Noah's college.

HARD TIMES

By Charles Dickens
New York: W.W. Norton, 2001

This story about rich and poor people takes place in Coketown, a manufacturing town in postindustrial revolution England. Wealthy Mr. Gradgrind is a cold and distant father to Louisa and Tom. Louisa marries Mr. Bounderby (twice her age) but is unhappy and leaves him after she realizes she married only to please her father. She is unlucky in love, just like Stephen Blackpool, a poor factory worker in the same town. Stephen loves Rachel, but he cannot marry her. The lives of all these characters cross when Stephen gets accused of robbing Bounderby's bank when in fact it was Tom who was responsible.

Economic Concepts in *Hard Times*

pp. 56–57, 60

Stephen wants to divorce his estranged wife and marry Rachel, the woman he loves and has been living with for many years. He believes his case is legitimate: his wife is a drunk who has abandoned him several times in the course of their nineteen-year marriage, stealing all his money each time she came back to him and then disappearing. However, Stephen does not understand the legal system and does not know how to go about getting a divorce. He is an illiterate factory worker and has no other options but to ask his boss for advice.

After a twelve-hour workday, Stephen is haggard and worn out when he walks up the hill to Mr. Bounderby's house. It is not common for a factory worker to visit his employer, but Stephen is desperate and takes a chance. At the door, a butler peers at him suspiciously. Before letting this unwelcome guest enter, he makes inquiries that reveal Stephen is a docile man who never makes trouble. He is allowed to proceed indoors to the room where Bounderby is eating cucumber sandwiches with his lemon tea.

There is ample evidence of unequal distribution of income and wealth in this selected passage of *Hard Times*. Neighborhoods are segregated by wealth: the rich, such as Mr. Bounderby, live in big imposing homes high up on the hill while Stephen and other factory workers live many to a room in the shacks below. Social customs underscore inequality: when Stephen finally gets to speak with Mr. Bounderby, he is not invited to sit down nor is he offered a drink, but rather, he stands respectfully, holding his hat in his hands, until he is dismissed. Language also differs by income category: Stephen speaks in ungrammatical sentences and has a limited vocabulary at his disposal while his boss's language reflects years of education. Finally, salutations reflect income categories: the wealthy are called by their name, preceded by the respectful term Mr. or Mrs. while factory workers have no name; they are merely called Hands, as that is what they are—hands that performs manual labor.

Yet one more distinction between income groups is revealed to Stephen when he visits Bounderby. The law is not the same for the rich and the poor. Stephen learns that in order to be granted a divorce, he has to make an appearance at the Doctor's Commons (the name for the law courts that have jurisdiction over divorce cases). Then, in order to register Rachel as his common-law wife, he has to make another appearance, this time at the Court of Common Law. Finally, Stephen has to appear in Parliament to obtain an Act of Parliament that enables him to remarry. In all three places, Stephen has to make a payment. In all three places, Stephen cannot enter unless properly dressed. Proper attire includes a suit, shirt, hat, and leather shoes, all of which Stephen does not own.

Bounderby leans back in his chair and says that the total cost of the right to marry Rachel would be between 1,000 to 1,500 pounds. Bounderby pauses and then adds, "Maybe twice that amount."

Stephen learns that poor working class individuals cannot obtain a divorce. In addition to all their numerous other hardships, poor folk also have to remain in failed marriages while the rich can use money to dissolve theirs.

Discussion Questions

1. Is it fair that Stephen cannot get divorced while Bounderby can? Is it fair that your neighbor went skiing over Christmas break and you had to work the night shift at Walgreens? Does fairness have anything to do with inequality?
2. Comment: The market economy is a great equalizer because when goods are available for sale, whoever has a demand for them can buy them so everyone gets what they want.
3. When people make grammatical mistakes and have a poor vocabulary, it is assumed that they are uneducated. Why is it often assumed that they must also be poor?

Chapter 32

Globalization

Film: *SYRIANA*
Fiction: *THE SISTERHOOD OF THE TRAVELING PANTS*

KEY ECONOMIC CONCEPTS

Most countries have open economies; that is, their economies are linked to each other through trade, foreign investment, capital flows, and the flows of workers across borders.

Foreign trade entails the outflow (*export*) and inflow (*import*) of goods and services. When exports are lower than imports, a country has a *trade deficit*. Some countries erect *barriers to trade* (such as tariffs) so as to decrease the quantity of imports. Such *protectionism* serves to protect some industries, albeit at the expense of others. When trade occurs, money flows across borders as payment. Since countries typically do not use the same currencies, traders must purchase *foreign currencies* at their market price (this price, determined by the demand and supply of the currency, is called the *exchange rate*).

Countries are also linked to each other through the flow of capital across borders. Such flows occur mostly when people or institutions in one country seek higher profits or higher interest rates than they can get at home. *Foreign financial investment* refers to the purchase of foreign bonds and stocks in search of higher interest rates while *foreign direct investment* entails investment in assets in countries where profit possibilities seem higher than at home. Firms that invest and operate abroad, also known as *multinational corporations*, are motivated by profit maximization.

The profits they make are then part of capital flows across borders (called the *repatriation of profits*).

In addition to goods and money, people also cross borders for a variety of reasons. The most important economic reason for *migration* is the movement of people in search of employment in the labor markets of another country.

Globalization refers to the integration of economies resulting from their trade, capital flows, and migration links. Such international integration seems to be growing and has led to economic interdependence among countries. Globalization is enabled in part by innovative technology that has decreased the price of global transportation and communication. It has also made the world seem smaller as people in remote corners of the world are now wearing similar clothes, surfing the same Internet sites, and talking to each other on cell phones.

SYRIANA

Rated R//2005/2hrs 8min/George Clooney, Matt Damon
Directed by Stephen Gaghan
Winner of Academy Award for Best Supporting Actor

This is a story of power in the oil industry. It is the post-Cold War period, and the United States is trying to obtain preferential access to Middle Eastern oil. A merger between two American oil companies is under scrutiny by government regulatory authorities. Bob Barnes (George Clooney) works for the CIA trying to manipulate politics and put friendly governments in power. His efforts are contrasted to those of a financial analyst, Bryan Woodman (Matt Damon), who is genuinely concerned with the economic development of his client's country. This political thriller combines politics, power, and petroleum with love and tragedy.

Economic Concepts in *Syriana*

Scene 20 (0:59–3:34)/Minutes 1hr 16:38–1hr 19:13

Once upon a time, in an unnamed Middle Eastern kingdom, two brothers vie for secession to the throne. The Sheik is ailing and following his death, the kingdom will move in one of two directions, depending on which son prevails.

In a poignant scene, the reform-minded Prince Nasir discusses his country's economic future with Bryan, the country's financial adviser. Nasir has lofty goals for his country. He wants to simultaneously introduce far-reaching political and economic changes. His progressive ideas were born during his studies at Oxford and Georgetown, and now he dreams of introducing democracy to his country. He wants to give women the right to vote; he wants to introduce a parliamentary system and an independent judiciary (Bryan nods while listening to Nasir, thinking how globalization has enabled the flow of ideas across borders).

By investing in infrastructure and capital projects, Prince Nasir expects economic development will occur. The money for that investment must come from oil exports, as that is the predominant output of his country. According to the prince, the entire oil industry, from drilling to marketing, needs to be reevaluated and updated. For example, Nasir wants to build a petroleum exchange in the Middle East where buying and selling takes place, cutting out the middlemen (who are always foreigners). He asks rhetorically why most oil exchanges are in London and New York, places that don't produce oil. Nasir wants to bring efficiency and profit maximization to the oil industry. One way to do this is to sell oil to the highest bidder, not to someone already grandfathered in. Prince Nasir already took a step in this direction when he recently signed a contract with a Chinese multinational corporation. It provided the highest bid on drilling rights and so was awarded an oil project. The Chinese are aggressive bidders in an effort to penetrate global markets, further proof of how globalization is bringing new players into global economic relations.

Bryan listens to Nasir with both admiration and skepticism. They both know that in order to bring his lofty plans to fruition, a new leadership must be installed in the kingdom. Those new leaders must sever ties that have a negative impact on their economy. That includes ties to American multinational corporations and the U.S. government.

As indication of how detrimental those ties are to his kingdom, Nasir tells an anecdote. Recently the U.S. president called up his father to say that there was unemployment in Kansas, Texas, and Washington. He asks the Sheik for his help in stimulating the economy. The Sheik comes up with a rescue package that includes a large purchase of American airplanes. Such Middle Eastern demand for American exports represents foreign trade that will stimulate employment in the United States as workers are hired to produce the airplanes. In turn, the income these workers receive will be spent on cars, toothpaste, and lawyers. The airplane exports and the secondary round of economic activity they engender will undoubtedly stimulate economic growth at home.

Why does the Sheik come to the assistance of the U.S. president? The answer lies in a debt he incurred years ago, during the Cold War, and has to do with his ascension to the throne. In repayment for a service rendered to him by the U.S. government, the Sheik signs away oil rights to

American multinational companies. That allows American companies to engage in direct foreign investment in the Middle East and reap the lucrative benefit of the flow of goods and money across the two countries' borders. They repatriate their profits without ever reinvesting them in the local economy. The ruling family shares huge profits with the American companies and, in the process, amasses great wealth, little of which benefits the local population.

Prince Nasir wants to sever those ties that are a stranglehold on the kingdom. He wants trade to be free from the barriers imposed by the political hold the United States has on his father. Nasir believes the political debt of long ago has been repaid, many times over. These are now new times with new players that have new goals and values.

Nasir's brother Prince Meshal disagrees with him. He has no motivation to sever ties with the American companies that have made him rich. He has no desire to share the oil revenues with the general population. Meshal is a jet-setter whose interests are limited to living the great life and is threatened by his brother's revolutionary ideas.

During a scene in *Syriana*, Nasir nods in the direction of a room full of people who disagree with him: his brother, his cousins, and a posse of lawyers who represent American oil interests. With a heavy heart, he tells Bryan that they are all pressuring the ailing Sheik to invalidate the contract with the Chinese. Bryan remains silent. He knows what the outcome will be. In his capacity as financial adviser to many Middle Eastern countries, he has seen a similar scenario play out over and over again.

Discussion Questions

1. Prince Nasir claims that modern history, from Versailles (the Treaty of Versailles, 1919) to the first Gulf War, was all about oil and Western countries' struggles to control Middle Eastern oil fields. What kind of control is Prince Nasir referring to? What is likely to happen to oil prices in the country that controls the oil fields?

2. In a sign of globalization, events in one part of the world are related to events in another (for example, in *Syriana*, unemployment in Kansas and the Middle Eastern purchase of American airplanes are related). Explain how cheap labor in Bangladesh is related to the closing of a shoe factory in Minnesota.

3. Ninety percent of the world's remaining oil is in the Middle East. In the absence of a major change in U.S. energy policy, it is in the American interest to ensure Middle Eastern economies are open to foreign investment by multinational corporations. Explain.

THE SISTERHOOD OF THE TRAVELING PANTS

By Ann Brashares
New York: Delacorte Press, 2001

Brigitte (the athlete), Lena (the beauty), Tibby (the rebel), and Carmen (the one who cares) are high school friends. They are about to go off in different directions for the summer when one of them buys a pair of pants that looks great on each one of their very different bodies. The four friends make a decision to share the pants while they enjoy their summers separately. Each girl gets to use them for a few weeks and then sends them on to the next friend. Through this one pair of jeans, the four friends remain bonded to each other while they are apart, and each girl's summer adventures are experienced through the traveling pants.

Economic Concepts in *The Sisterhood of the Traveling Pants*

pp. 143–144

Lena is visiting her grandparents on the Greek island of Santorini. It is her first trip abroad and although people speak a language she doesn't know (Greek was not offered at her high school), Lena is amazed at how many things are the same as back home. She drinks Coke, brushes her teeth with Colgate, and washes her clothes with Tide while the radio plays familiar American tunes. She travels thousands of miles and still finds products she buys in her local supermarket. As part of globalization, multinational corporations have built distribution networks that have enabled their products to permeate local markets across the world.

Although Lena is currently in possession of the Traveling Pants, it is time to send them on to the next recipient, her friend Tibby. She packs them into a small bundle (even though they are jeans, they are not the stiff kind) and heads through the town's narrow cobble-stoned streets toward the post office.

Lena pays for postage with Greek drachmas, not American dollars. In fact, everything she purchased since her arrival to Greece has been paid with drachmas. Lena had changed her U.S. dollars into drachmas at a bank soon after her arrival. It is likely that she inquired about the exchange rate between the two currencies in order to decide how many dollars to change. The price of drachmas is adjusted daily as it is a market price that fluctuates with the supply and demand of drachmas.

The Traveling Pants will leave Greece and reach the United States in approximately one week. The speed of their travel from origin to destination is an indication of the increasing linkages that connect countries across the globe in the twenty-first century. In contrast to bygone days when letters crossed the Atlantic Ocean by ship and took several months to arrive at their destination, today there are multiple daily flights that connect the two countries and carry mail in their baggage compartments. Lena and Tibby, as well as others who buy and sell and invest and travel across national borders, have become accustomed to the speed with which international exchanges take place.

By crossing a border to visit her grandparents, Lena became an international tourist. She is part of a growing number of people who travel for leisure (as well as business) at a time when globalization has made faraway places more accessible than before. Inexpensive air travel enables students like Lena to visit foreign countries and become exposed to different ways of doing things. Increased tourism thus leads to increased intercultural awareness.

One incident on Santorini highlights the dangers of not understanding other cultures. Lena had been skinny-dipping and then wore her Traveling Pants inside out. Both actions led her grandparents to erroneously accuse a neighborhood boy of something he didn't do. Fistfights took place, followed by the rupture of a decades-old friendship among neighbors. It all happened because of a misunderstanding based on cultural differences and accentuated by the language barrier.

The incident highlights how important it is, in our modern interconnected world, to know each other's customs and languages. Numerous international political incidents might be avoided if we have greater knowledge of the ways of other cultures.

Discussion Questions

1. The island where Lena's grandparents live is, according to myth, the place where Atlantis was located before a powerful volcano eruption made it disappear under water in 1630 BC. Imagine that one day technological innovation enables tourist excursions to the underwater civilization. What happens to the demand for Greek drachmas? What happens to its exchange rate relative to dollars?
2. Imagine: Lena forgets to pack her sunglasses. She goes to a Greek shop to buy a replacement. In the United States, she had paid $65 for her Ray-Bans while in Santorini they are priced at the equivalent of $95. Using key concepts, explain what might account for that difference in price.
3. Although Lena speaks no Greek, it is likely that she will learn some by the end of the summer. Why might speaking a foreign language be useful in her future job search?

Chapter 33

Command Economies

Film: *RED CORNER*
Fiction:
ONE DAY IN THE LIFE OF IVAN DENISOVICH

KEY ECONOMIC CONCEPTS

In *market economies*, households and firms, through supply and demand, determine prices and therefore also determine the allocation of economic resources.

Command economies, also known as centrally planned economies, are those in which directives for micro and macro level economic activity come from the government. *Central planning* determines what will be produced and how (as opposed to prices determining what is produced and how, as happens in a market economy). Government ownership of firms and enterprises is the norm, rather than private ownership. In addition to holding property rights, governments also control and manage all economic activity.

The United States does not have a pure market economy. Rather, it has a *mixed economy*, one in which the market predominates, although there is some government involvement in the allocation of resources and in ownership.

During much of the twentieth century, both China and the Soviet Union had command economies and were ruled by communist parties. Now both countries have mixed economies in which the market plays a dominant role (China is, however, still ruled by the Communist Party). In Cuba and North Korea, command economic systems continue to prevail.

RED CORNER

Rated R/1997/ 2hrs 2min/Richard Gere, Bai Ling
Directed by Jon Avnet

Although China is still a communist country, its economy has opened up to international business. Jack Moore (Richard Gere) is an American attorney who travels to Beijing to negotiate the first TV satellite joint venture. Soon after his arrival, a woman he befriended ends up dead, and he is accused of murder. Moore is incarcerated and is appointed an attorney by the court, Shen Yuelin (Bai Ling). She is willing to represent him even though it is still dangerous to associate with foreigners (and Americans are particularly suspicious). The struggle between old communist ways and the new economic openness is evident as Yuelin and Moore together show how and why he was framed.

Economic Concepts in *Red Corner*

Scene 1 (1:40–3:00)/Minutes (1:40–3:00)
Scene 2 (0:00–1:45)/Minutes (3:00–4:45)

It is the mid-1990s when Jack Moore arrives in Beijing to begin trade negotiations with the Chinese government. He is scheduled to meet with high-ranking members of the Ministry of Radio, Film and Television. In order to get there, Moore drives through Beijing in an automobile provided by the U.S. Embassy.

The drive takes him through Tiananmen Square, the scene of recent political protests against the Chinese leadership. It takes but a few moments for Moore to realize the monitoring presence of the Chinese government. Although long dead, Chairman Mao's face covers red posters affixed proudly to the walls of the Forbidden City. Soldiers in formation march with imposing strides, and all across the square, monitoring cameras are attached to lampposts. When Moore looks out of his open window, a camera rotates to hone in on him. Big brother is watching. It is 1997 in China, and the Communist Party is still firmly entrenched in the political life of its citizens.

The Party is also entrenched in the economy, although there are signs that its reins are loosening. Globalization has not bypassed China, as evidenced by the beginnings of international trade and financial flows across its borders. Moore's mission is part of this trend. If he succeeds in negotiating the deal outlined in his briefcase, the U.S. entertainment industry will have a foothold in the world's largest market of viewers—well over one billion people.

The purpose of today's meeting with the folks at the Ministry of Radio, Film and Television is for Moore to lay out the entertainment package he seeks to export to China. As is common in command economies, it is the Chinese government that will import, purchase, and control distribution of all foreign television programs. The government monitors are closely involved because television programs are potent—they can change the hearts and minds of the population and for that reason are viewed as a potential threat.

Moore is given the opportunity to show clips of the television shows he is promoting. He is under extra pressure to make a good impression since a German entertainment package is also under consideration. Such competition is an indication of a market, one in which there is supply by at least two producers of entertainment and demand by the Chinese government.

The room is darkened and the screen lights up. The show is called *Beachside* (it is a knockoff of *Baywatch*). Members of the Chinese ministry, together with government-appointed censors, watch bikini-clad American beauties emerging from the water, their hair dripping wet and suntan lotion glistening on their exposed skin. Minutes into the program, the Chinese translator tells Moore that American programs are pornographic, violent, and superstitious. Wisely, Moore does not negate the allegation. Instead, he disarms the censors by quoting Chairman Mao, first in broken Chinese, and then in English: "Use the West for Chinese purposes." He adds his interpretation: If programs teach people that America is violent, wouldn't that discourage your people from pursuing Western values?

Given that the goal of government censorship is to control exposure of the Chinese population to those Western ideas they might then want to emulate, Moore cleverly provides a way for the Chinese to buy his product while believing it to be safe. Although the censors in the Ministry of Radio, Film and Television are impressed that Moore can quote their revered leader, the battle with the Chinese government is just beginning.

Discussion Questions

1. *Red Corner* was filmed in 1997 at a time when the Chinese economy was bursting onto the world stage. After a series of reforms that moved China towards a market system, China is now one of the fastest growing countries in the world (its GDP grew by over 10 percent in 2006). Which elements of a command economy do you think were replaced by the reforms?
2. Censorship is not limited to communist China. Can you think of examples of censorship in the United States, a democratic country with a mixed economy?

3. On film, Richard Gere tries to bring about change in China. In real life, he is actively involved in the liberation of Tibet, a part of China. He joins other celebrities with missions, such as Angelina Jolie (concerned with African child refugees) and Princess Diana (who sought to have land mines banned). How might celebrity involvement help or hinder change within a repressive country?

ONE DAY IN THE LIFE OF IVAN DENISOVICH

By Aleksandr Solzhenitsyn (winner of 1970 Nobel Prize in Literature
New York: Farrar, Straus and Giroux, 2005

Ivan Denisovich Shukhov is an inmate in Siberia, having been accused of political crimes. He is a fictional representation of one of the eighteen million citizens of the former Soviet Union who spent time in the notorious work camps set up by Stalin during 1929–1953. The book tells stories about why and how Shukhov and his fellow inmates have been imprisoned. They all receive censored letters from their families, which they share with each other and through which they learn about life outside, under communism. By comparing life outside to their life inside the camps, inmates realize that there is little difference.

Economic Concepts in *One Day in the Life of Ivan Denisovich*

pp. 62–63

Ivan Denisovich Shukhov is always cold and hungry as there is insufficient heating in the prison camp and insufficient food to properly feed all the inmates. In addition, Shukhov is also always scared since he doesn't know why he is imprisoned or how long he is expected to stay in this remote Siberian camp. In the beginning of his incarceration, Shukhov often thought he would wake up and find himself back on his farm, relaxing after an abundant harvest, waiting for his rotund wife to place a bowl of steaming borscht before him. Now, nearing his tenth year in the camp, Shukhov wonders daily if he will die before his wrongful imprisonment is righted.

Shukhov is assigned to work on a power station in a field, open to the elements. Even though the temperature often reaches -40 degrees Fahrenheit, inmates are expected to work outdoors. When assigned to a construction site, they must work quickly lest the mortar freeze. Their clothes are always inadequate; their mittens always torn. Every morning they scramble for boots from a messy pile and inevitably end up with the wrong size.

Under these conditions, the inmates have to perfect survival strategies. They plot and pray and trade and hoard. Although camp conditions are significantly more difficult than life on the outside, in some ways the camp is a microcosm of the Soviet economy. Shukhov's camp for political prisoners is owned and operated by the central government. It is like an enterprise insofar as it uses inputs to produce output. The principal input is labor—it is the one most abundantly available. It is forced, meaning that workers have no choice about offering their labor to the workplace. The manual laborers manufacture, construct, and maintain, depending on the season and the regional demands (Shukhov describes one such camp, whose inmates built the Belomor Canal linking the Baltic to the White Seas when there was a strategic need for such a canal). Output produced by the inmates becomes a part of the national product market as well as a part of the circular flow of economic activity.

As in any enterprise, whether in a market or command economy, labor productivity is crucial in determining output. In Shukhov's prison camp, each inmate is pressured to produce to the maximum of his ability. For example, Pavlo, the deputy foreman urges Shukhov and his twenty-three squad members (called the Gang 104) to work quickly and to produce more, always more. His motivation to increase productivity is due to the Prison Reward System, which rewards prisons that reach output goals set by the government. Shukhov describes how such monetary rewards are then distributed through the prison hierarchy so that he and his fellow inmates receive only an increase to their food portion of 200 grams of bread. The prison administrators receive the bulk of the reward.

Since the inmates are not free, their labor is free. In other words, inmates are incarcerated and the terms of their jail sentences include their free provision of labor. No wages are received. The inmates' only payment is food that is linked directly to their output. It follows that food is the price of their labor. The Soviet government sets prices of inmate labor inside prisons by setting the quantity of food given per output produced, just like it sets prices of shoes and newspapers outside prisons.

Prison output levels are set by the central planners in Moscow as they are for any Soviet enterprise. In a scene of *One Day in the Life of Ivan Denisovich*, Skuhkov describes his squad leaders' obsession with meeting prescribed output goals (in the book they are called percentages). Quality of output doesn't matter; exploitation of resources doesn't matter. The only thing that matters is achieving the percentages set forth by the central planners. Failing to do so results in punishment most strongly felt by those at the bottom of the hierarchy; similarly, succeeding in achieving prescribed percentages results in rewards least enjoyed by those at the bottom.

If the prison output were sold in a market economy, and if the labor input were hired in a market economy, then supply and demand, rather than government directive, would determine production. At the time of the Soviet forced labor camps, there were no such markets on a national scale. However, in *One Day in the Life of Ivan Denisovich*, there is evidence of limited micro-level market activity inside the prison as Shukhov engages in trade as well as barter. Given that he is both frugal and a hoarder, Shukhov often manages to save a bit of his meager food ration to trade at a future time (since food is a medium of exchange). Shukhov also barters his time: a fellow inmate, Tsezar, doesn't like to stand in line for morning boot assignment, so Shukhov stands for him in exchange for some rare treats that Tsezar's family sends in a monthly food package.

Discussion Questions

1. Why did food, rather than boots, become a medium of exchange in Shukhov's prison?
2. After the labor camps were closed in 1953, the Soviet government hired construction workers to build capital projects, such as canals. How was government expenditure affected? Does your answer depend on how the wages of workers are determined?
3. The United States is said to be a mixed economy. Can you think of assets that are owned and controlled by the government? What about assets that are either owned or controlled but not both?

About the Authors

Milica Z. Bookman is a professor of economics at Saint Joseph's University with some twenty-five years of teaching experience. She has published nine single-author books and one coauthored book as well as numerous chapters and articles in scholarly books and journals. Her books have received the Outstanding Book Award, and her book readings have been aired on C-SPAN. In 2002, she received the Tengelmann Award for Excellence in Teaching and Research. In addition, she has been a guest lecturer at the Woodrow Wilson Center, University of Pennsylvania, the U.S. Army War College, Foreign Policy Research Institute, and University of Miami, among others.

Aleksandra S. Bookman is a student at New York University with a major in history and a minor in film production. She studied economics at the London School of Economics and completed internships at NBC's *Saturday Night Live* as well as Sony BMG Music Entertainment. During the summer of 2008 she was a reporter/researcher for Miami.com, a culture and lifestyle website sponsored by the *Miami Herald*. Aleksandra presented *Economics in Film and Fiction* at two international academic conferences. In addition, she speaks five languages and has taken courses in Italy, Spain, and France.